Celtic Mandalas for the Soul

Including Inspiring & Beautiful Celtic Mandalas designs: Lotus, Sand, Flowers and Sun; a creative view of Universe's Circle.

Karthic Praveen

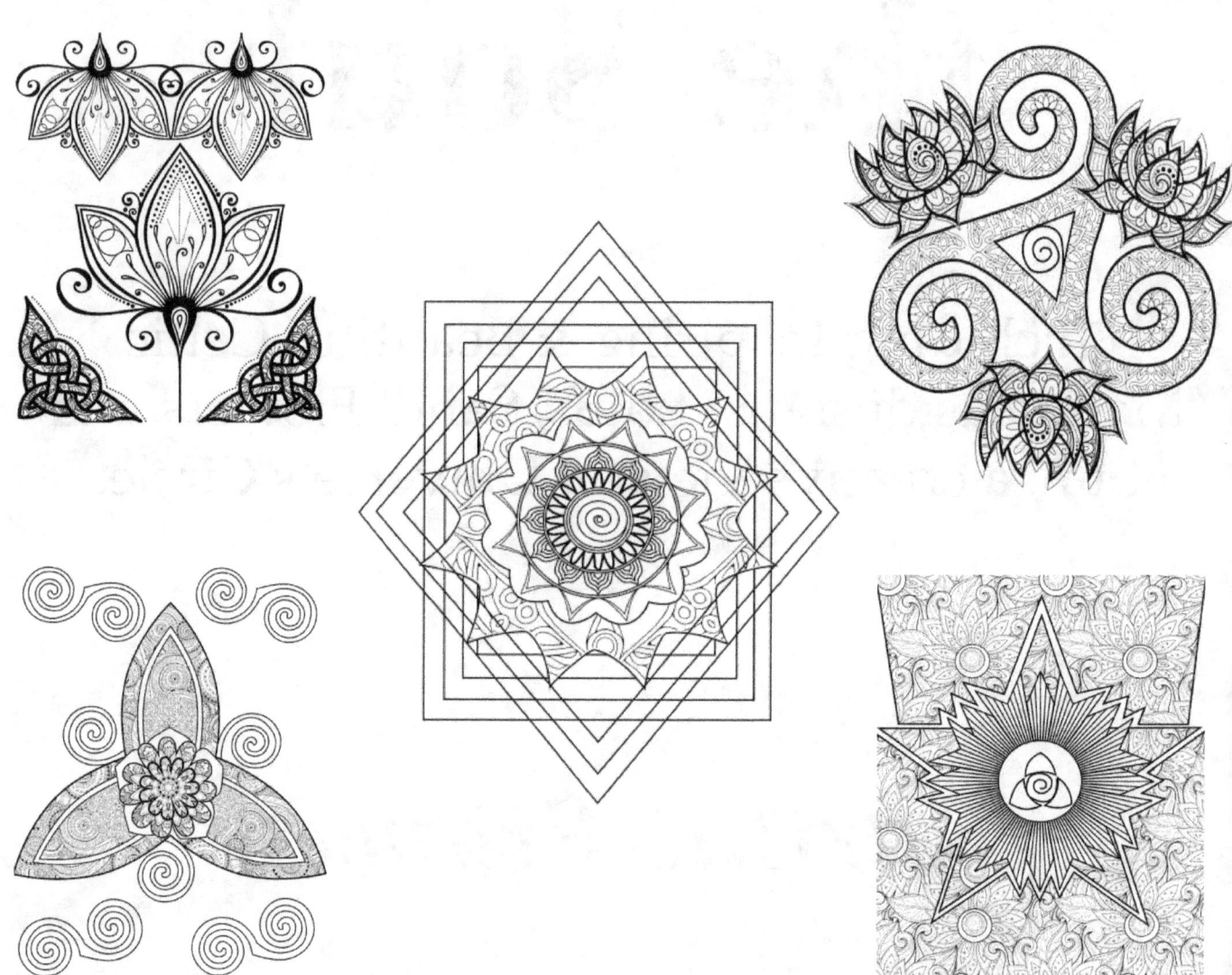

Introduction:

MANDALA means circle, Hindu and Buddhist religious traditions from India and Himalaya represent the spiritual universe trough this beautiful art.

Mandalas evoke the time as an eternal circle CREATION-FLOURISHING-DESTRUCTION-CREATION.

Celtic Mandalas for the Soul coloring book includes wonderful patterns designed to unleash your creativity while exploring:

❖ *Lotus Mandalas:* A flower that grows in shadow water, color it and think of enlightenment rising out of suffering and impurity.
❖ *Sand Mandalas:* Once completed sand mandala is destroyed evoking impermanence, color it to realize impermanence and then feel newly cleansed.
❖ *Flower Mandalas*: wildflowers with new unfold petals, while painting think about the deep inside meaning of colors and forms, essence beyond appearance.
❖ *Sun Mandalas:* Symbolize gold and represent the highest purity of possible state of being, create it and focus on the radiant light of transformation.

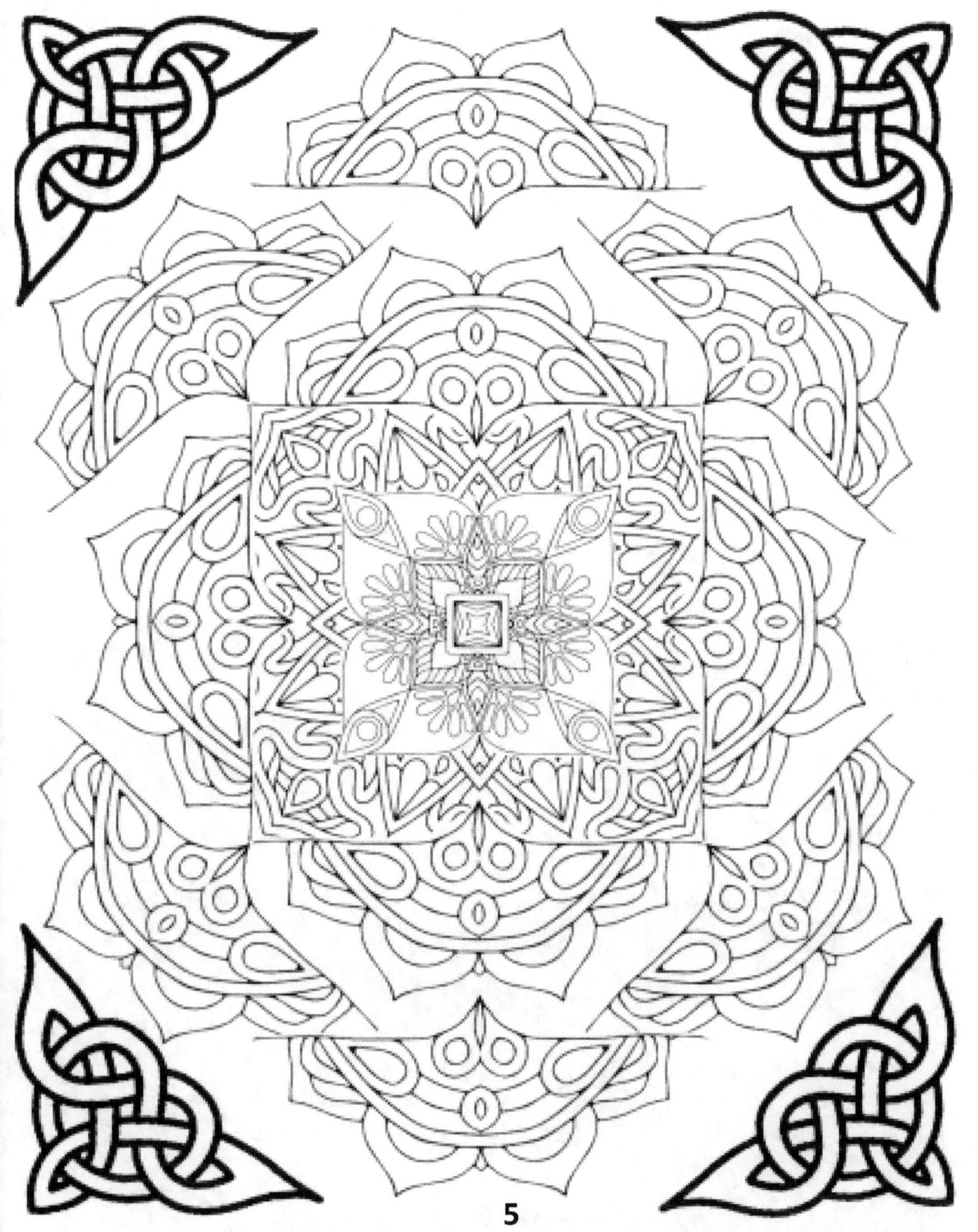

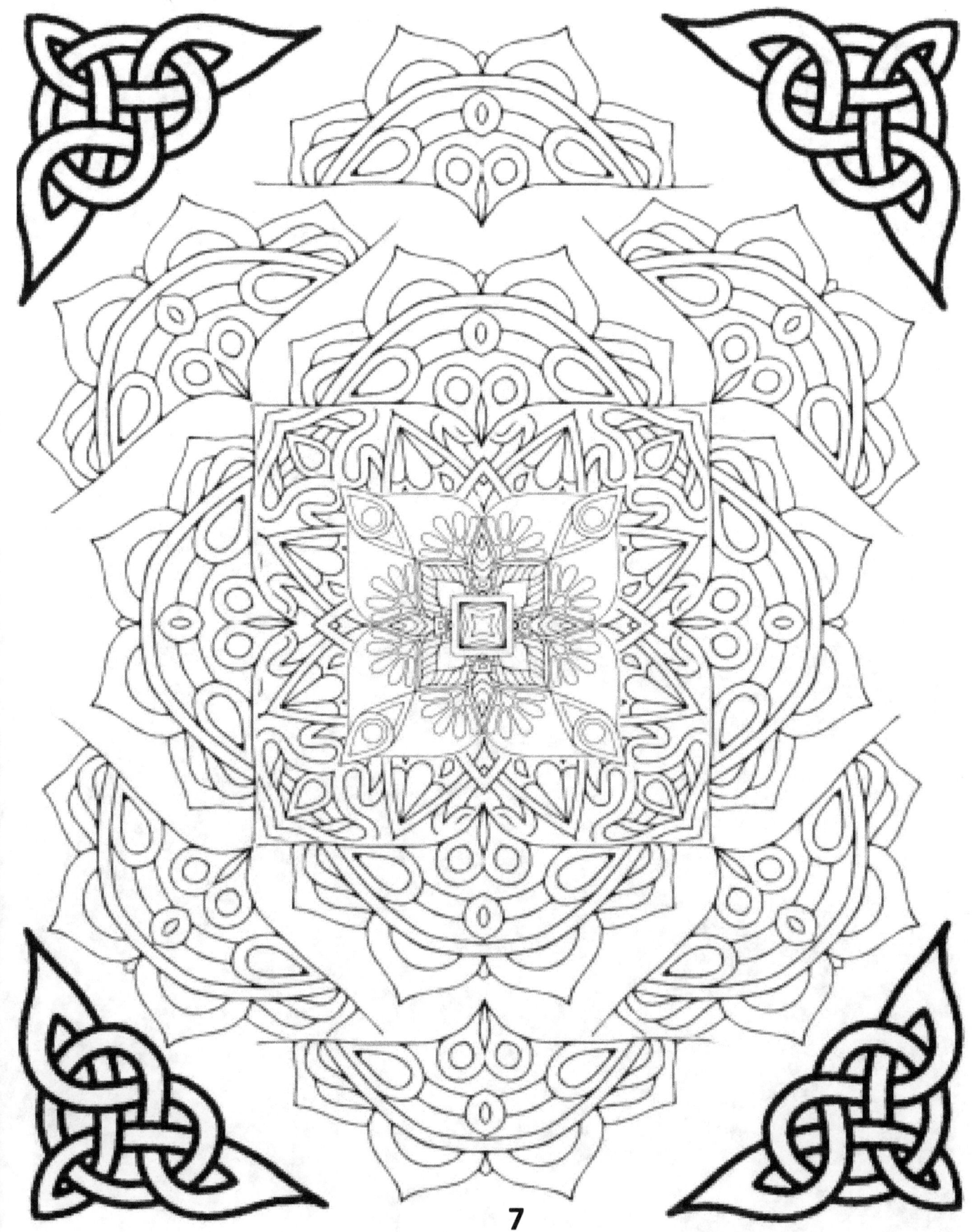

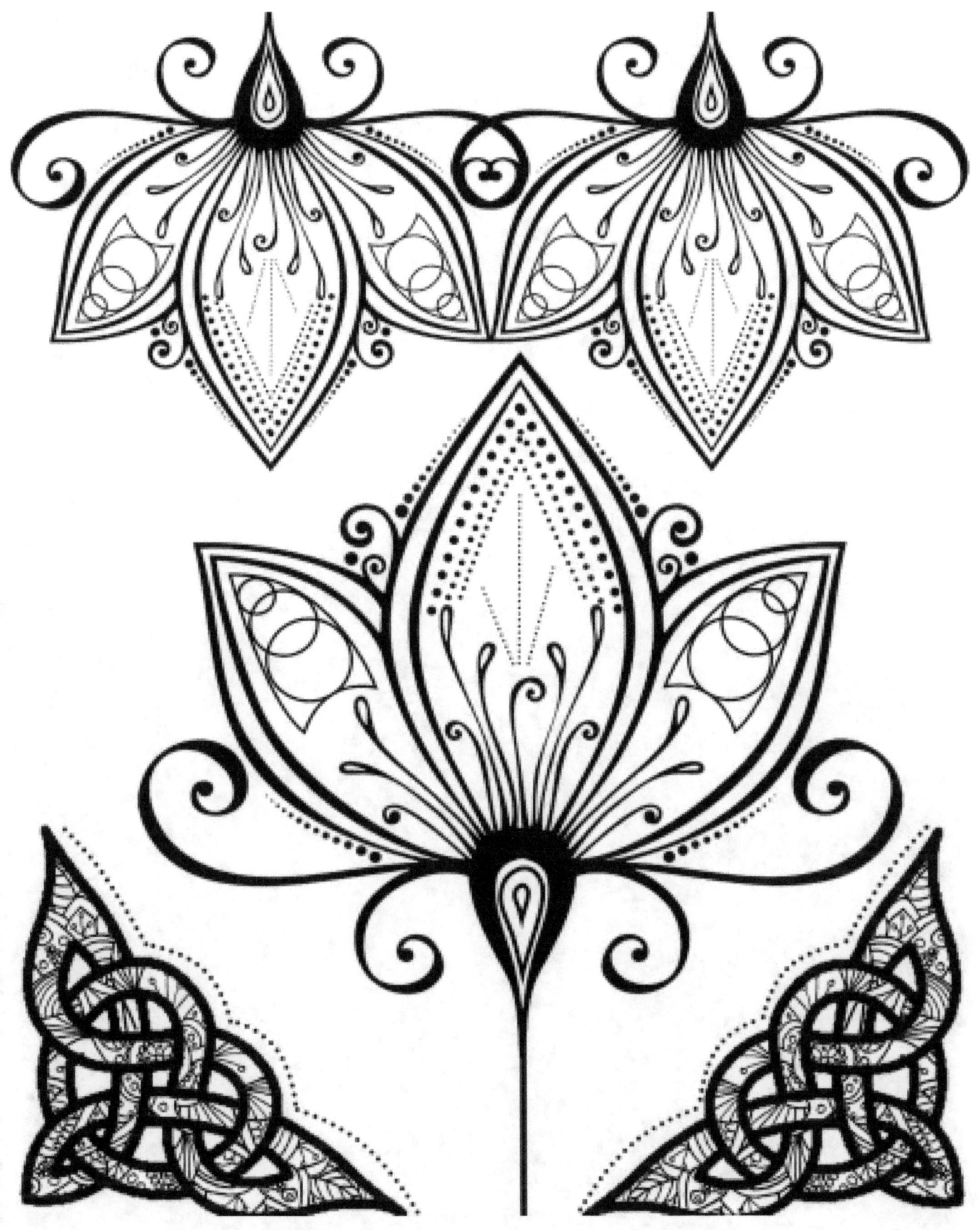

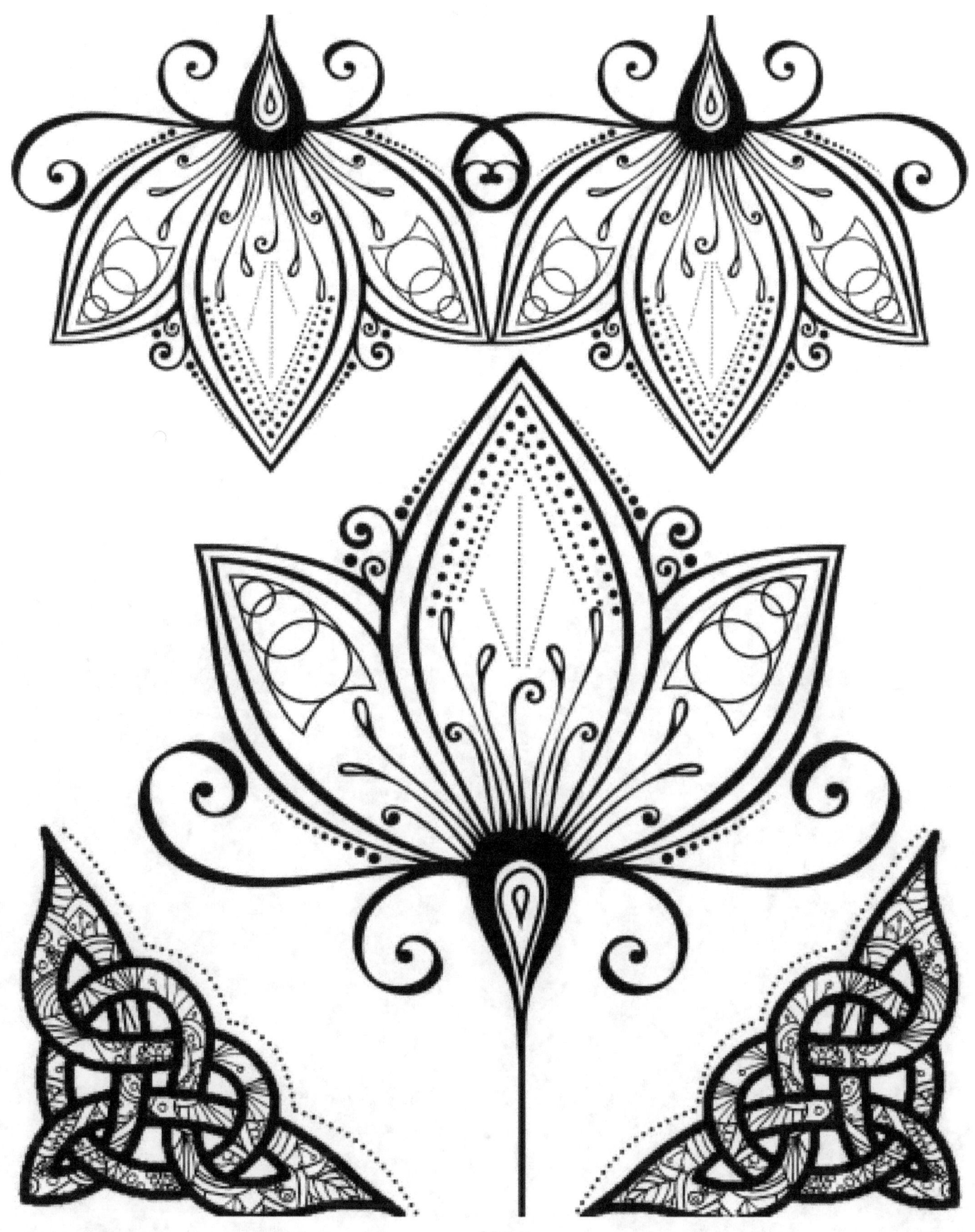

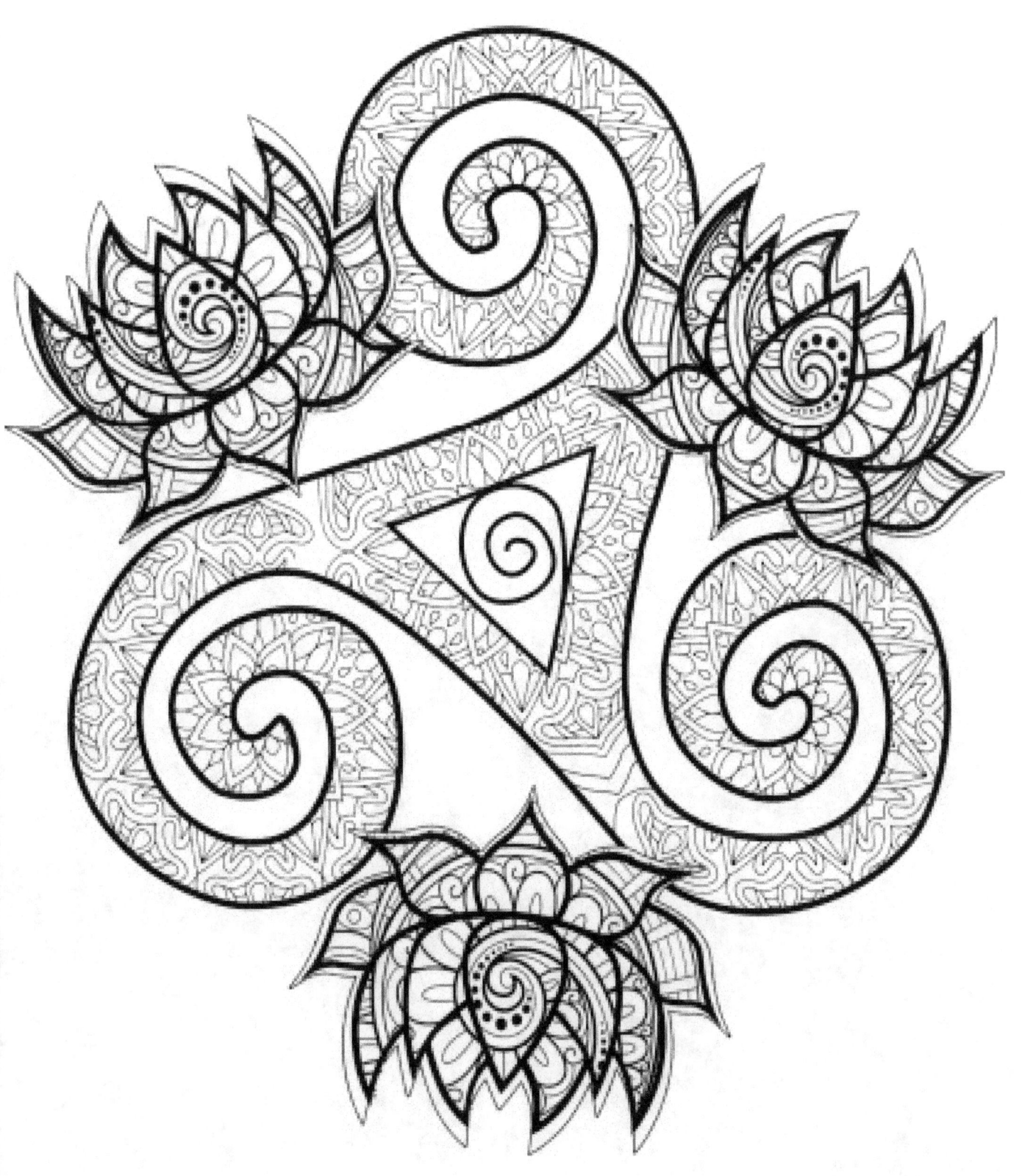

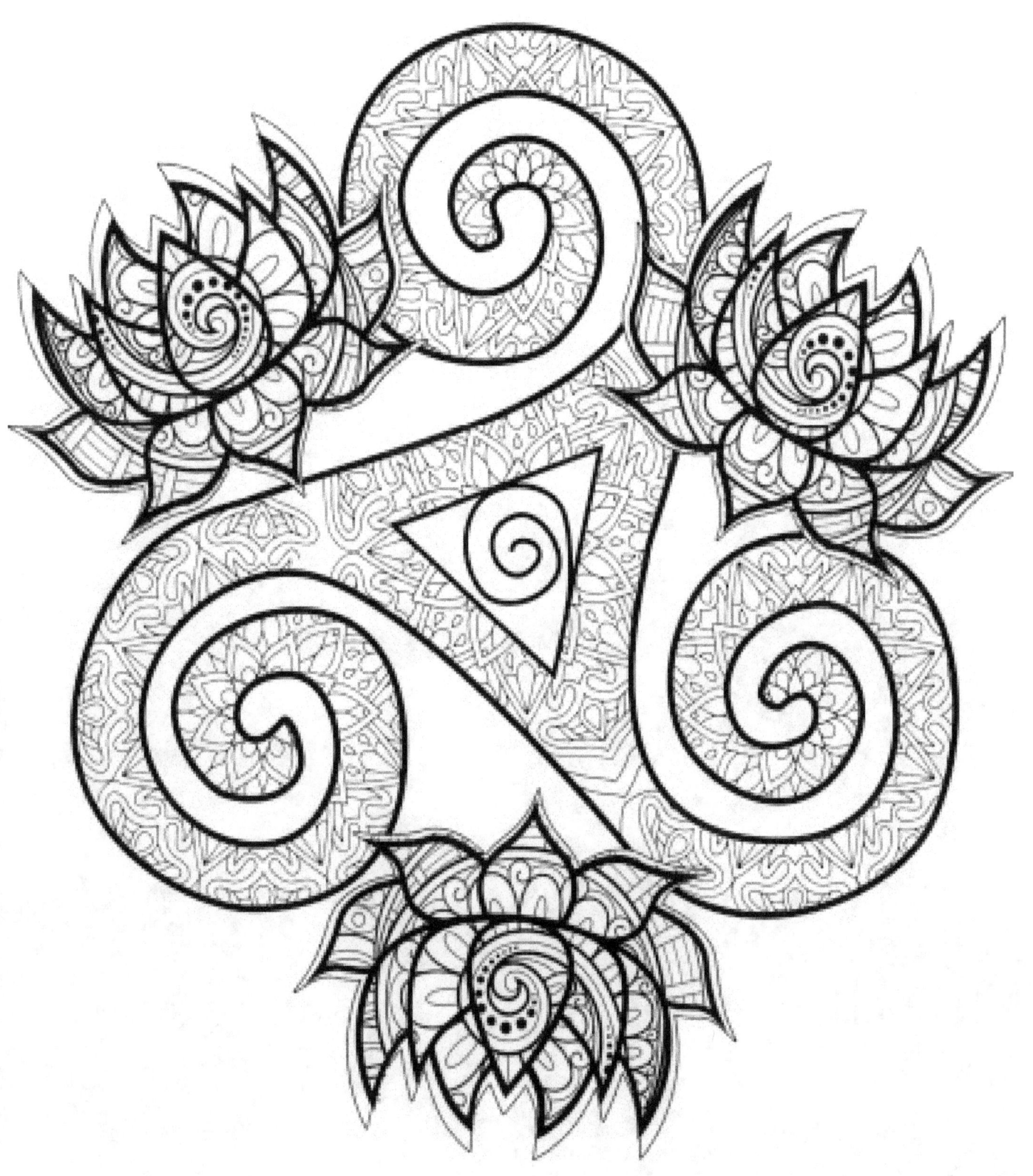

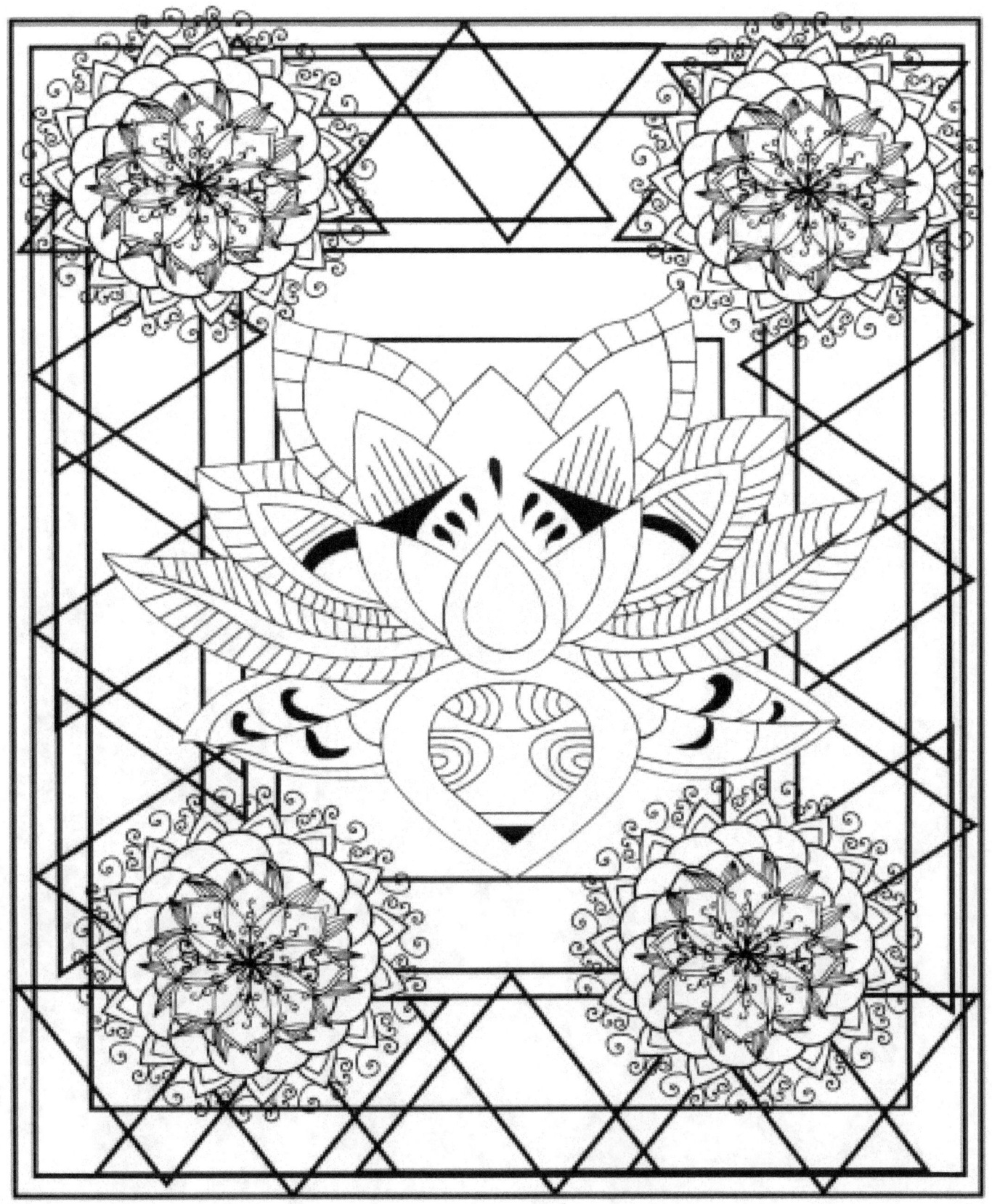

18

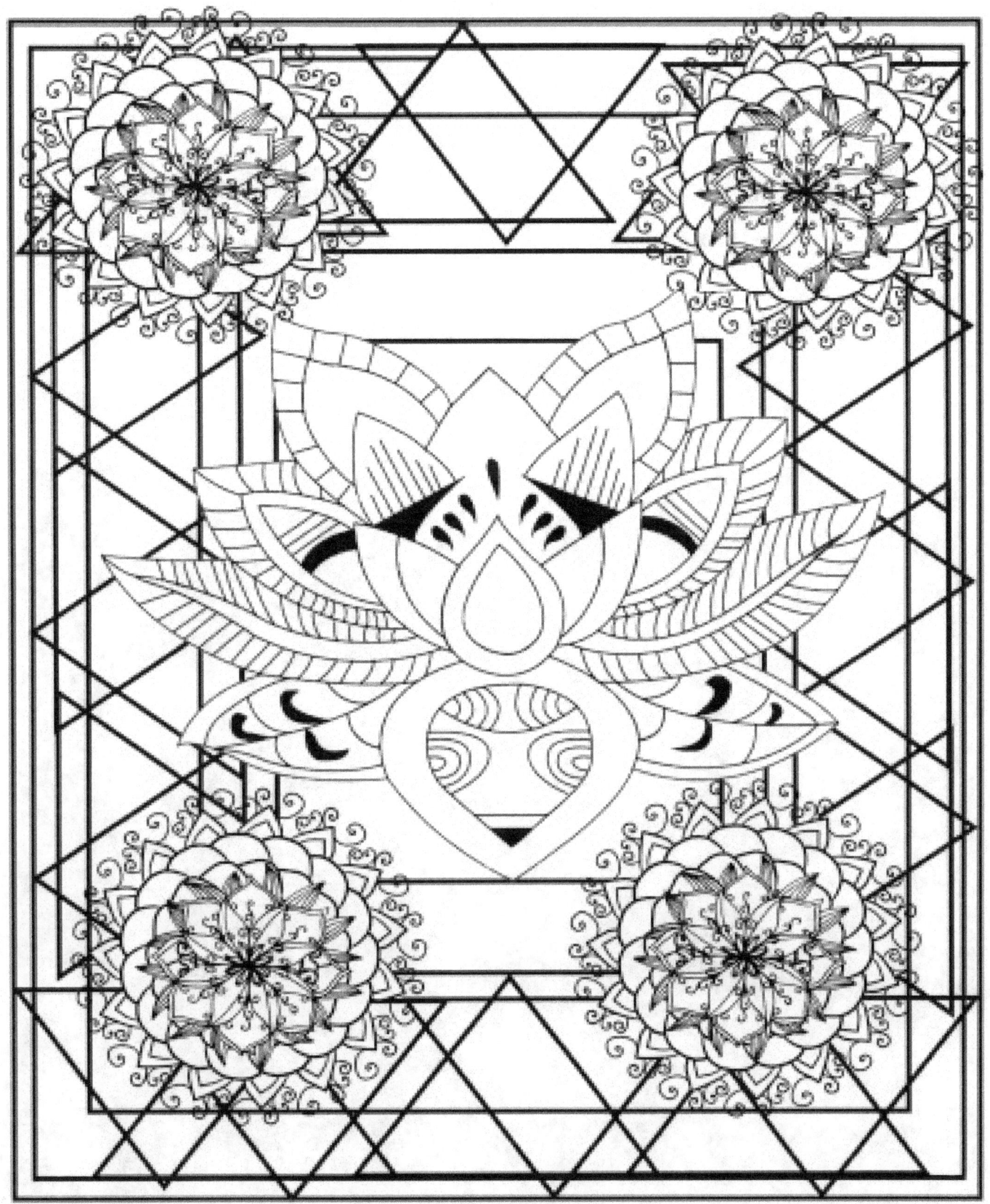

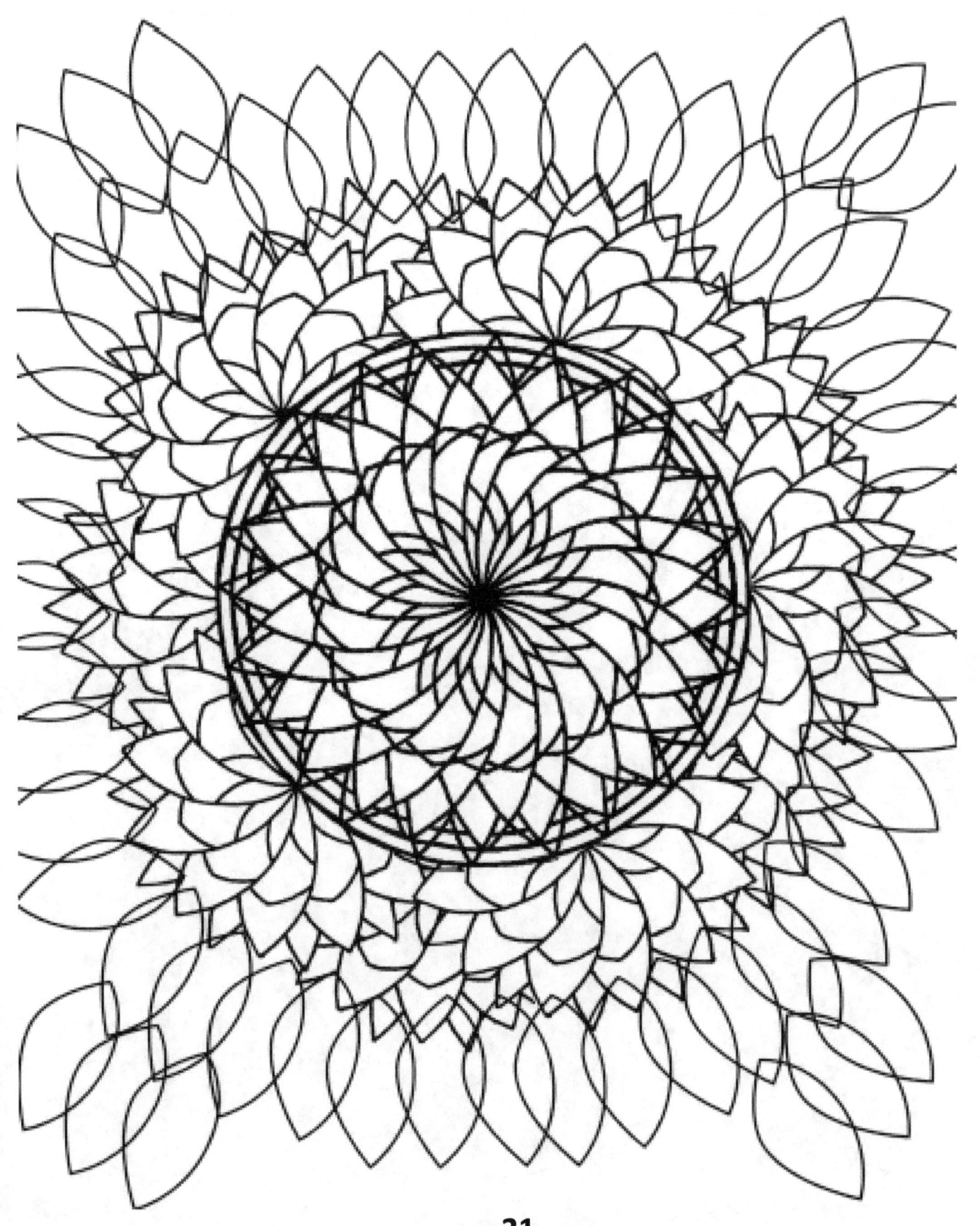

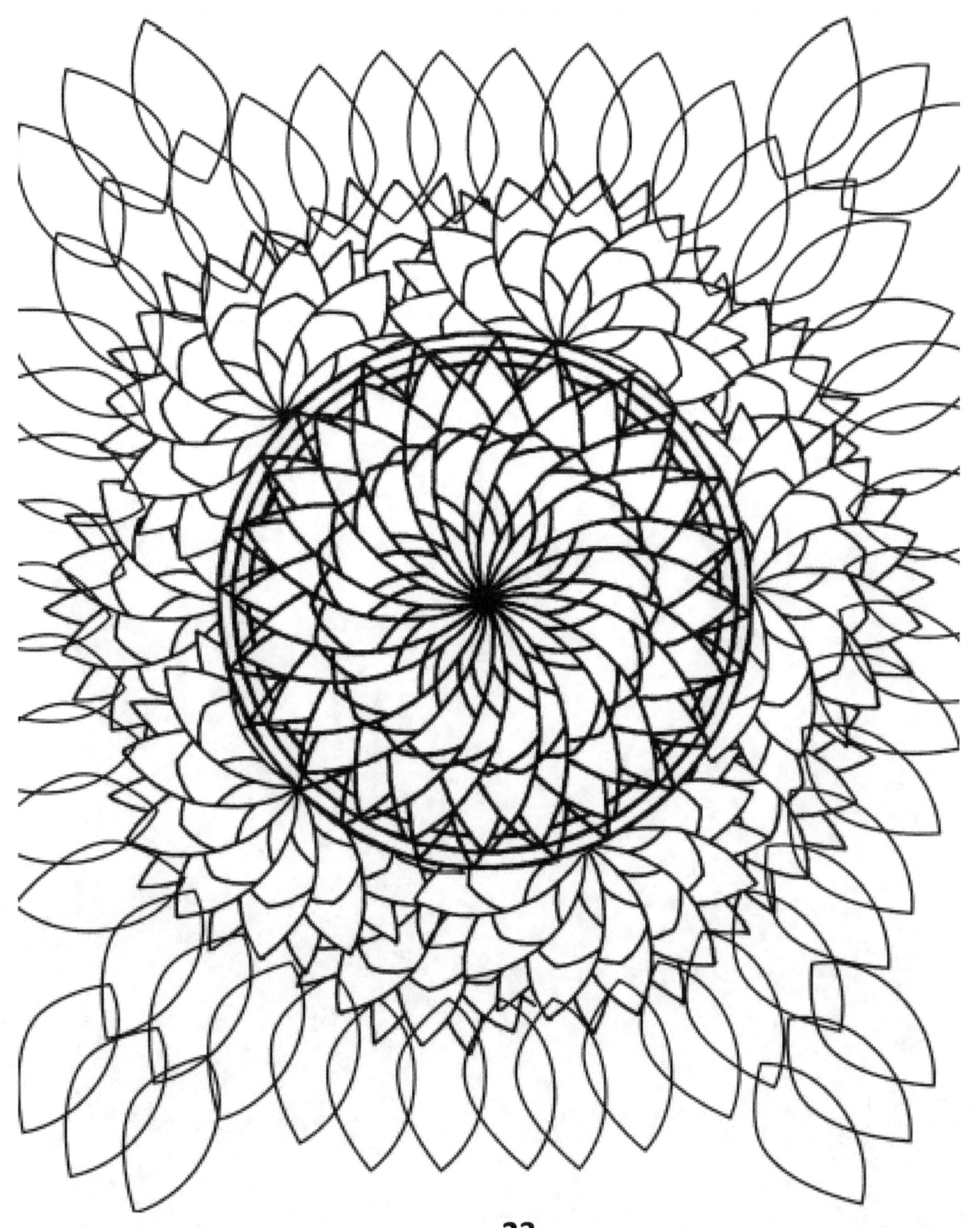

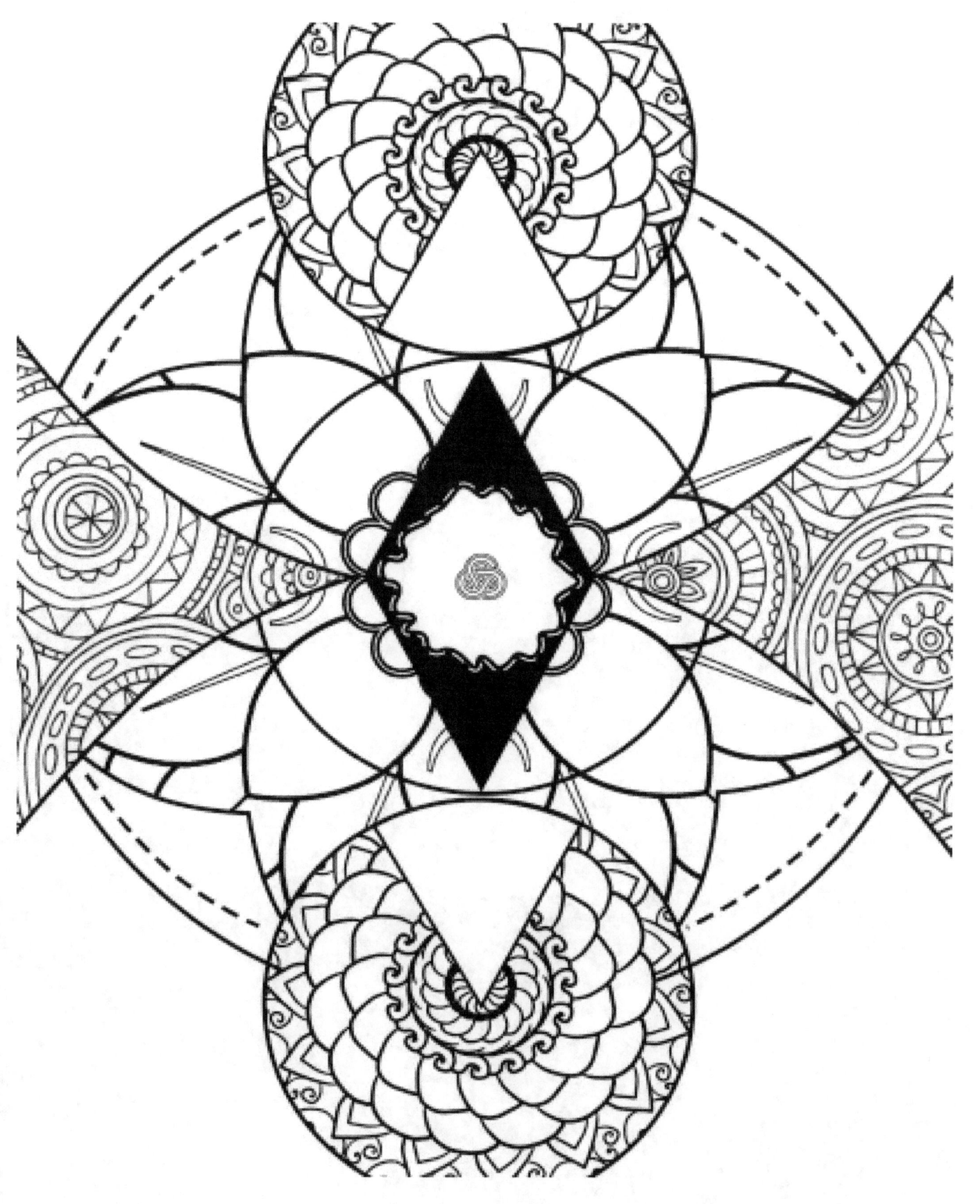

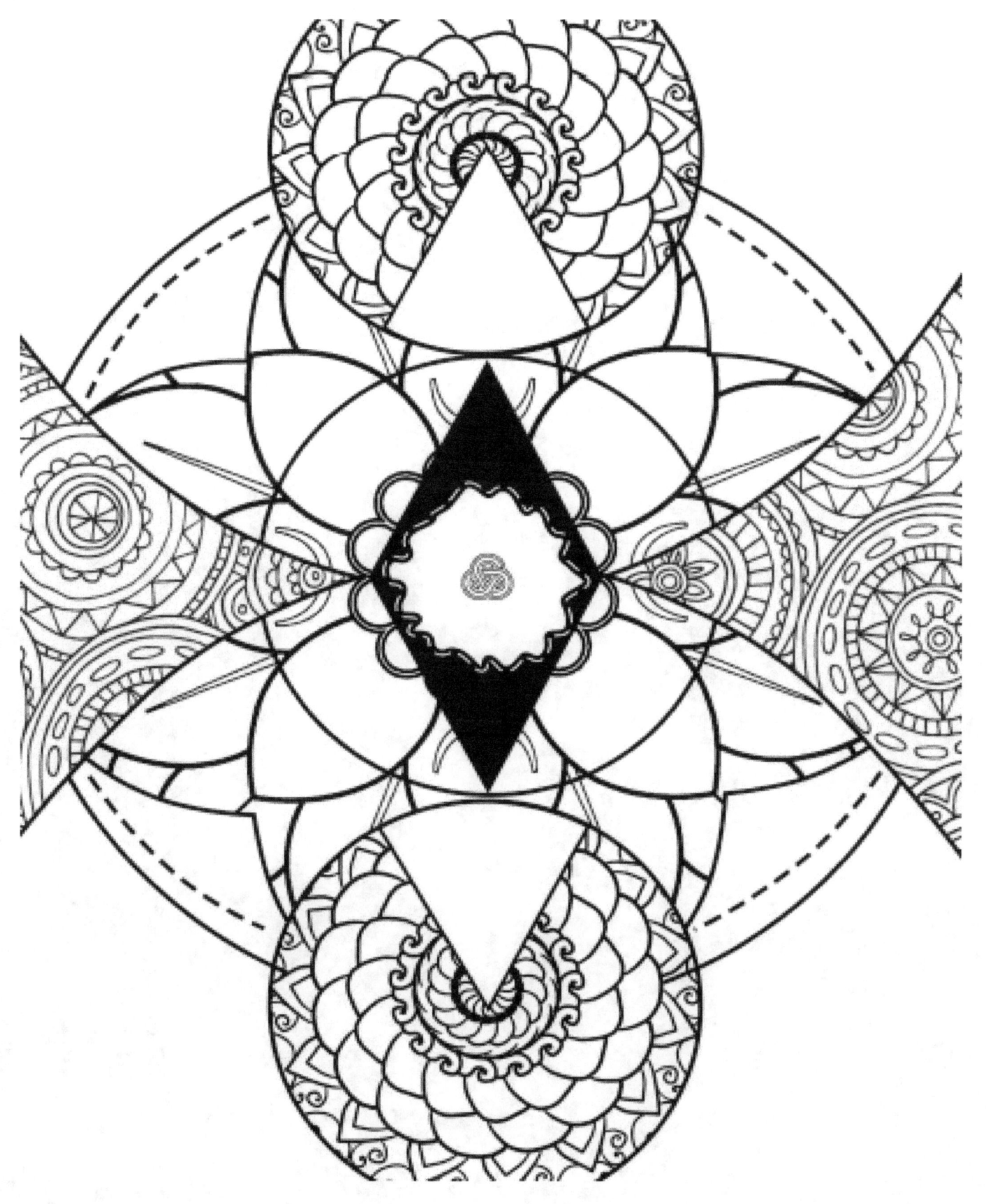

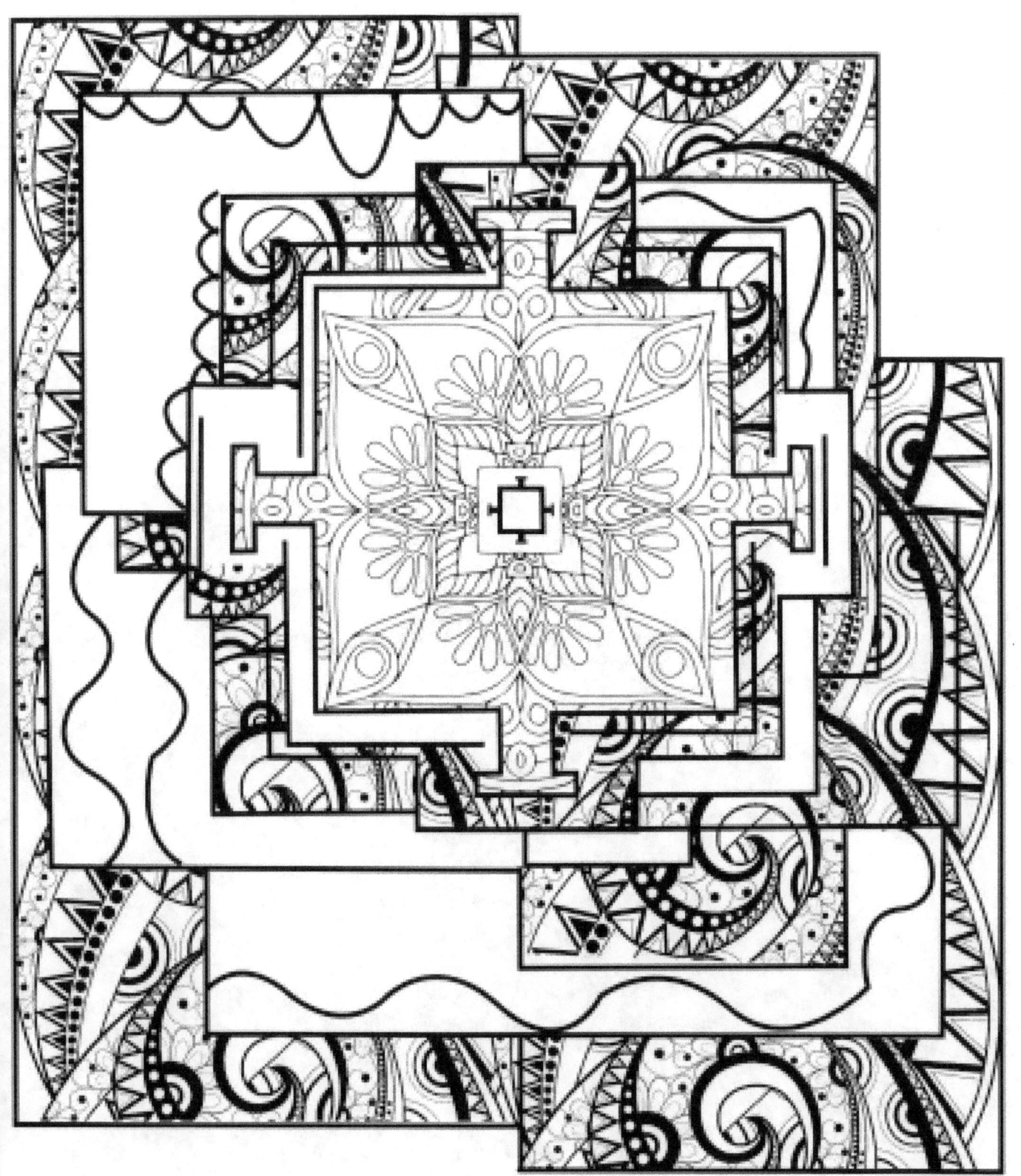

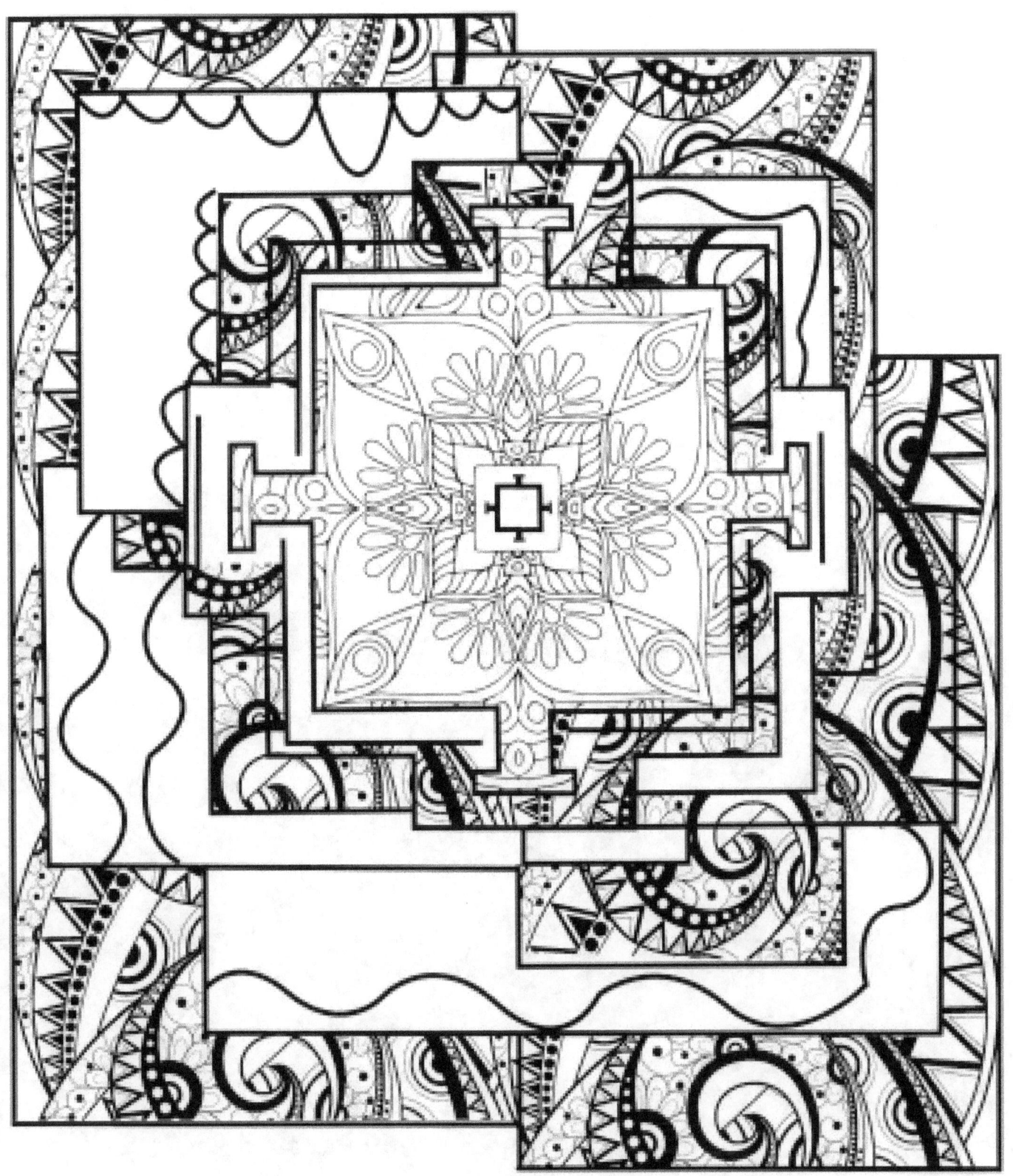

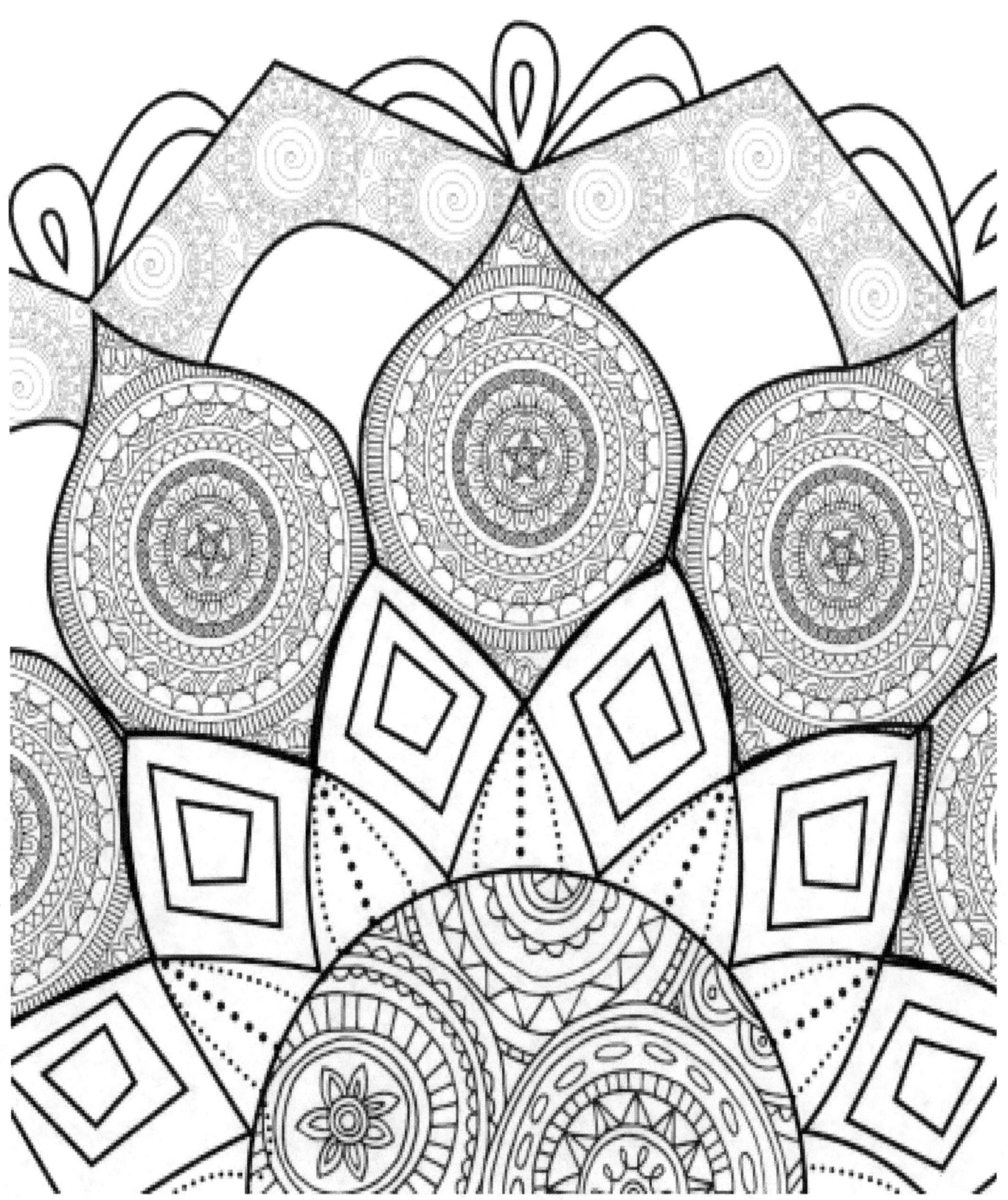

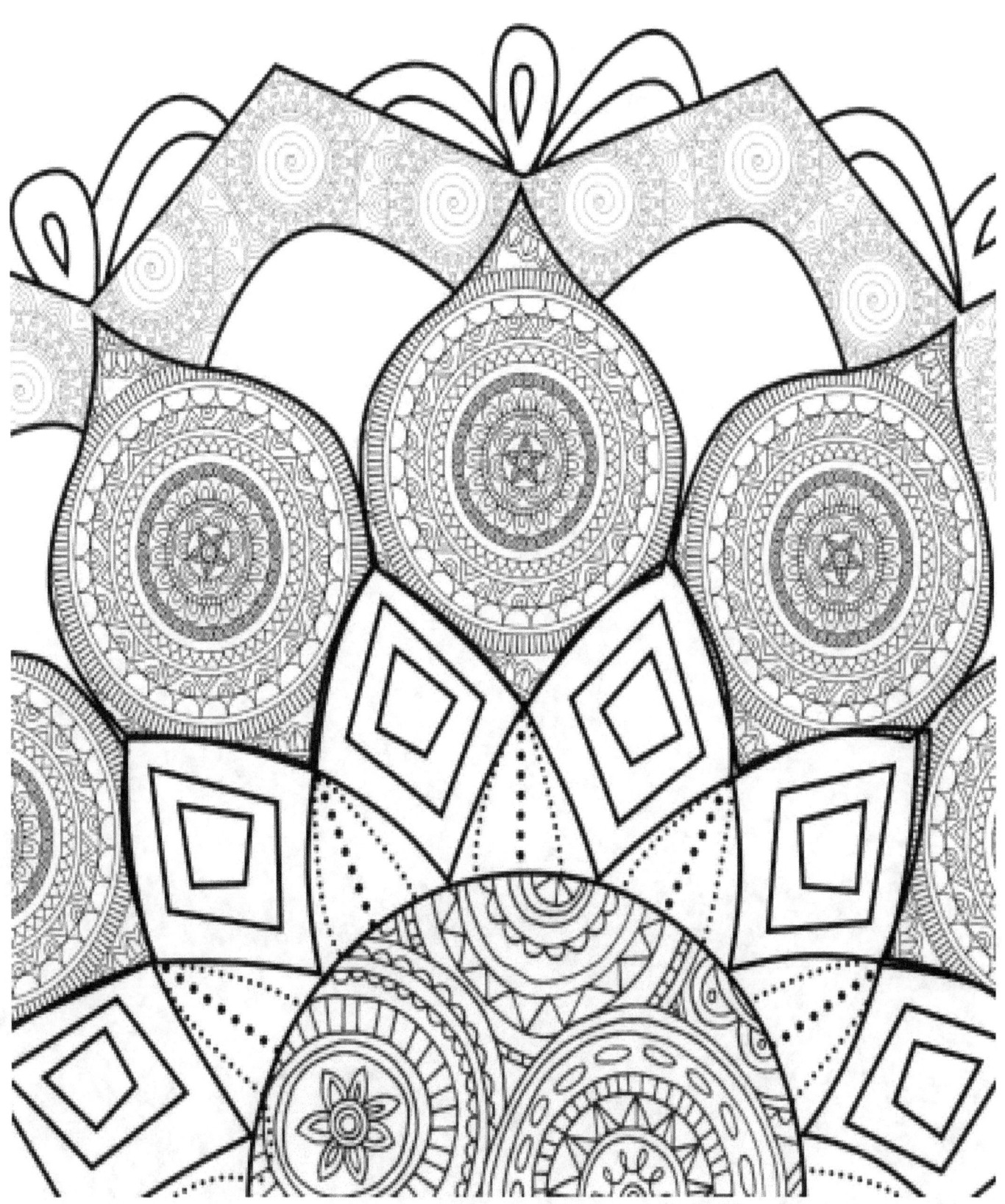

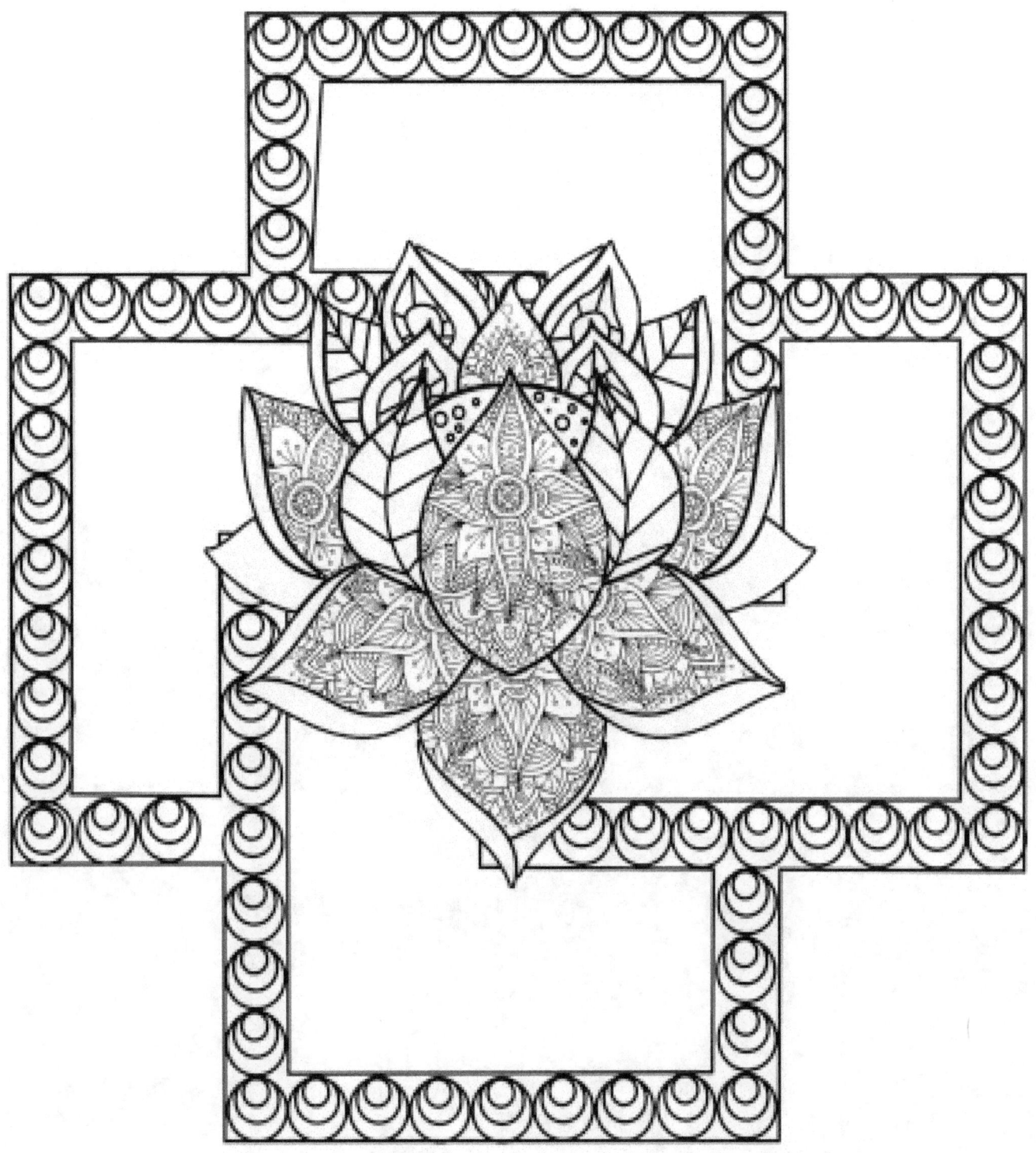

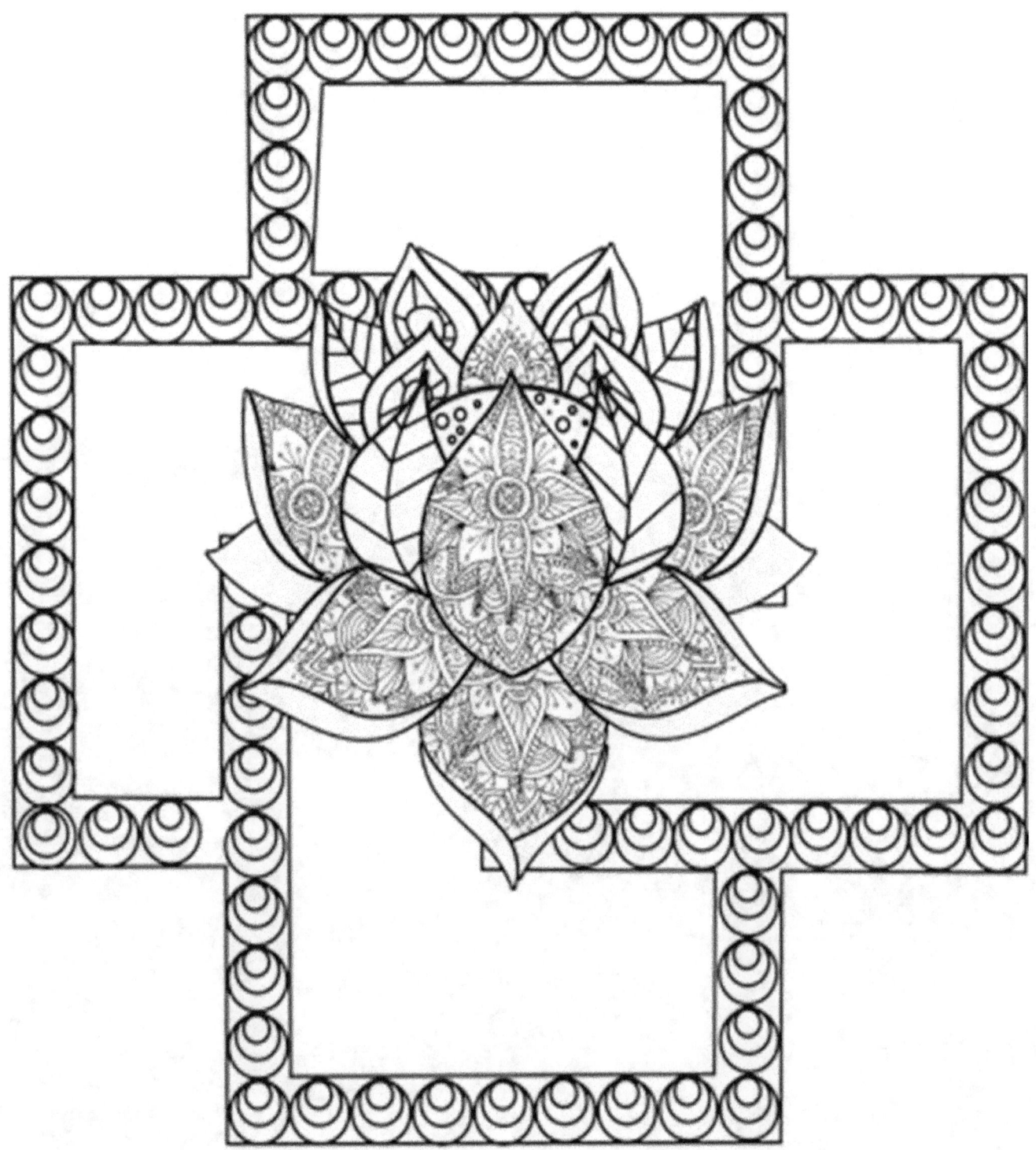

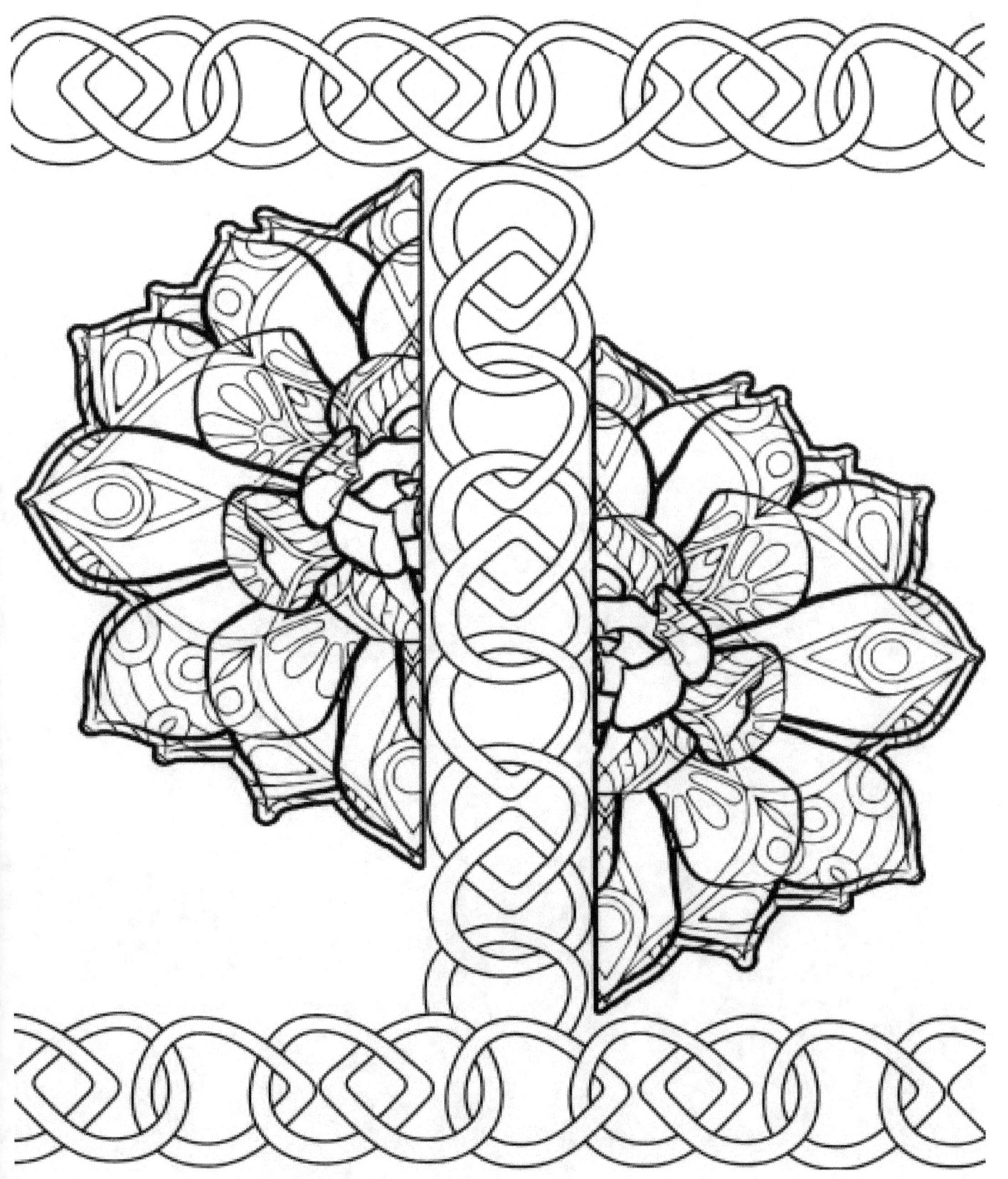

41

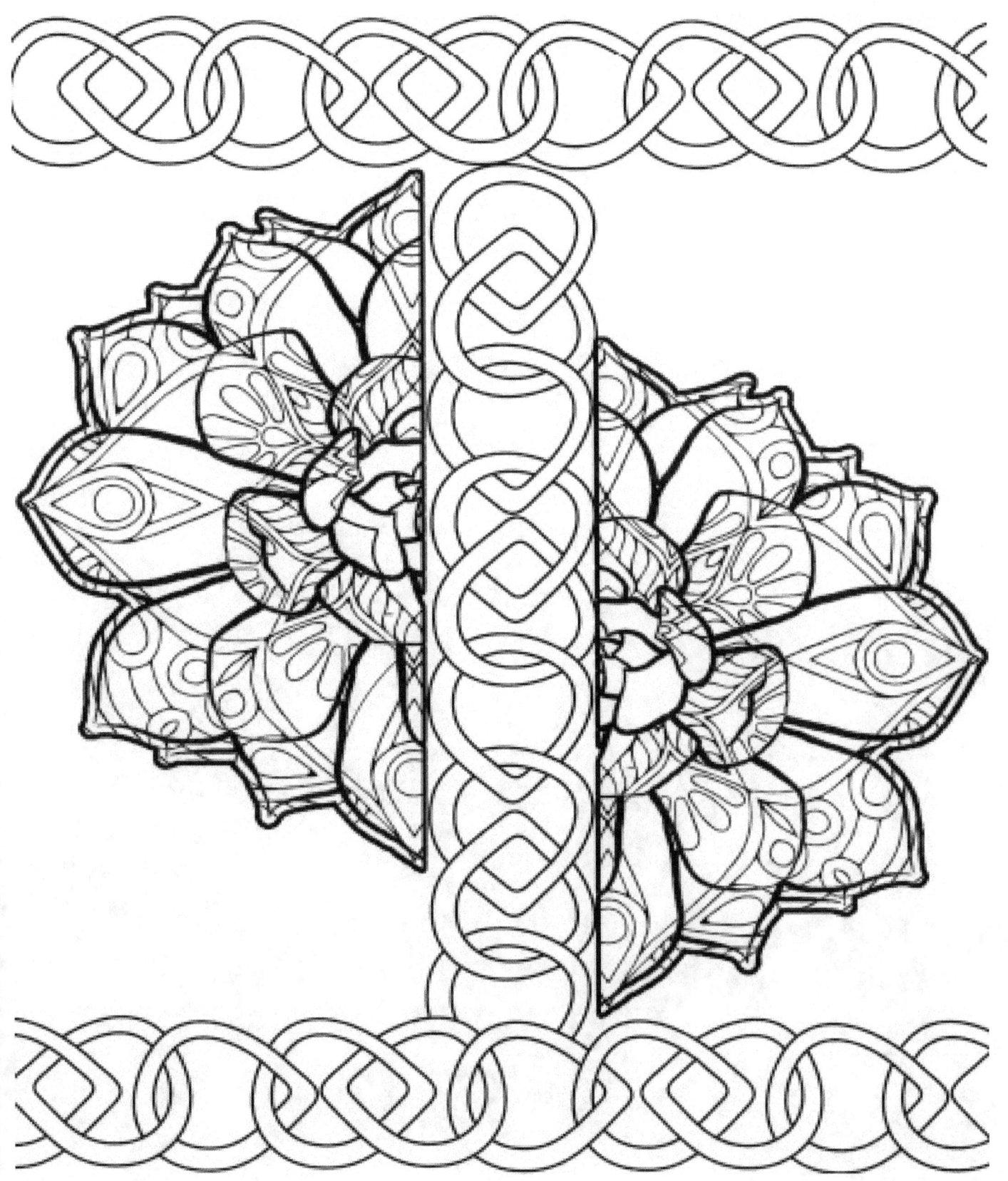

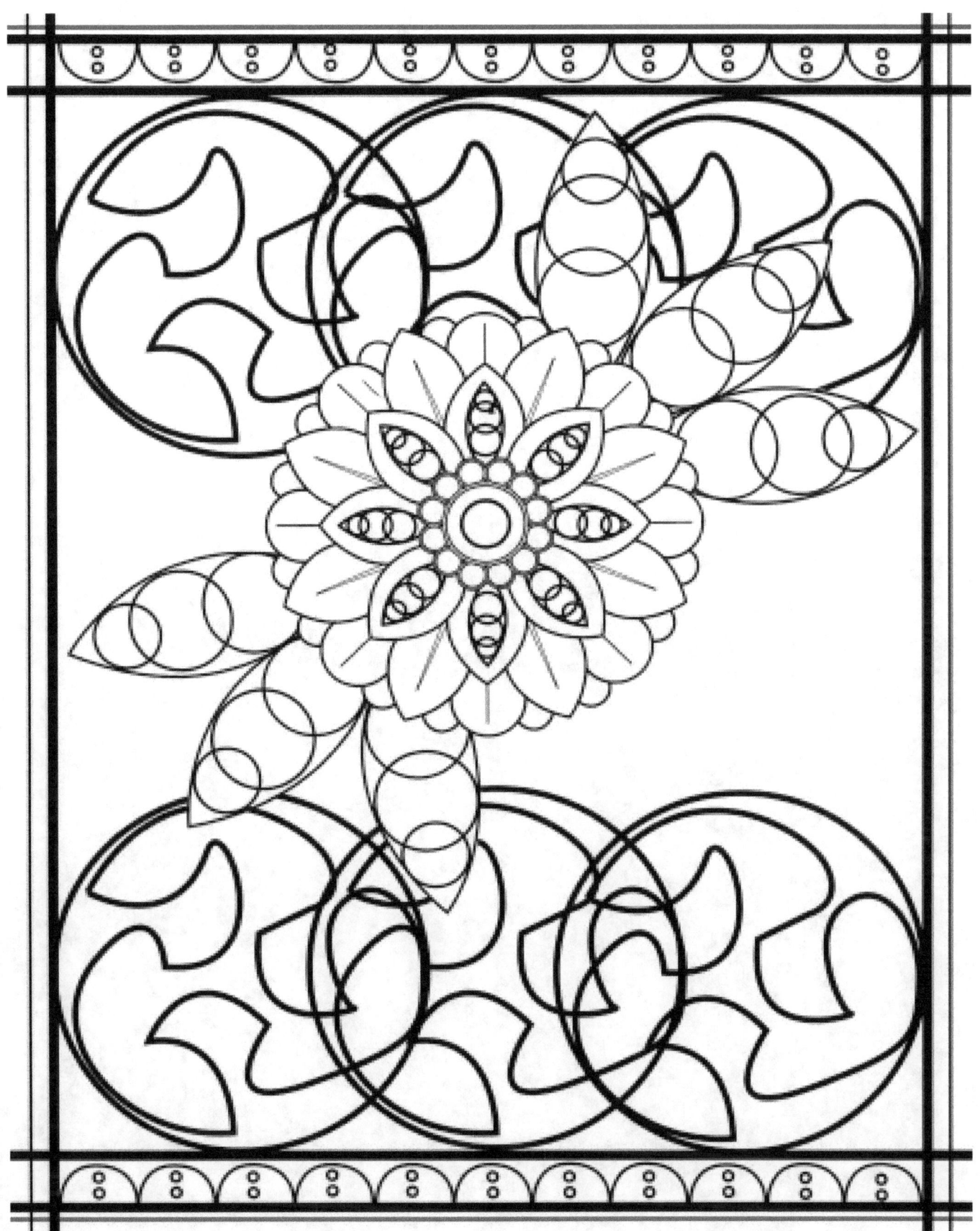

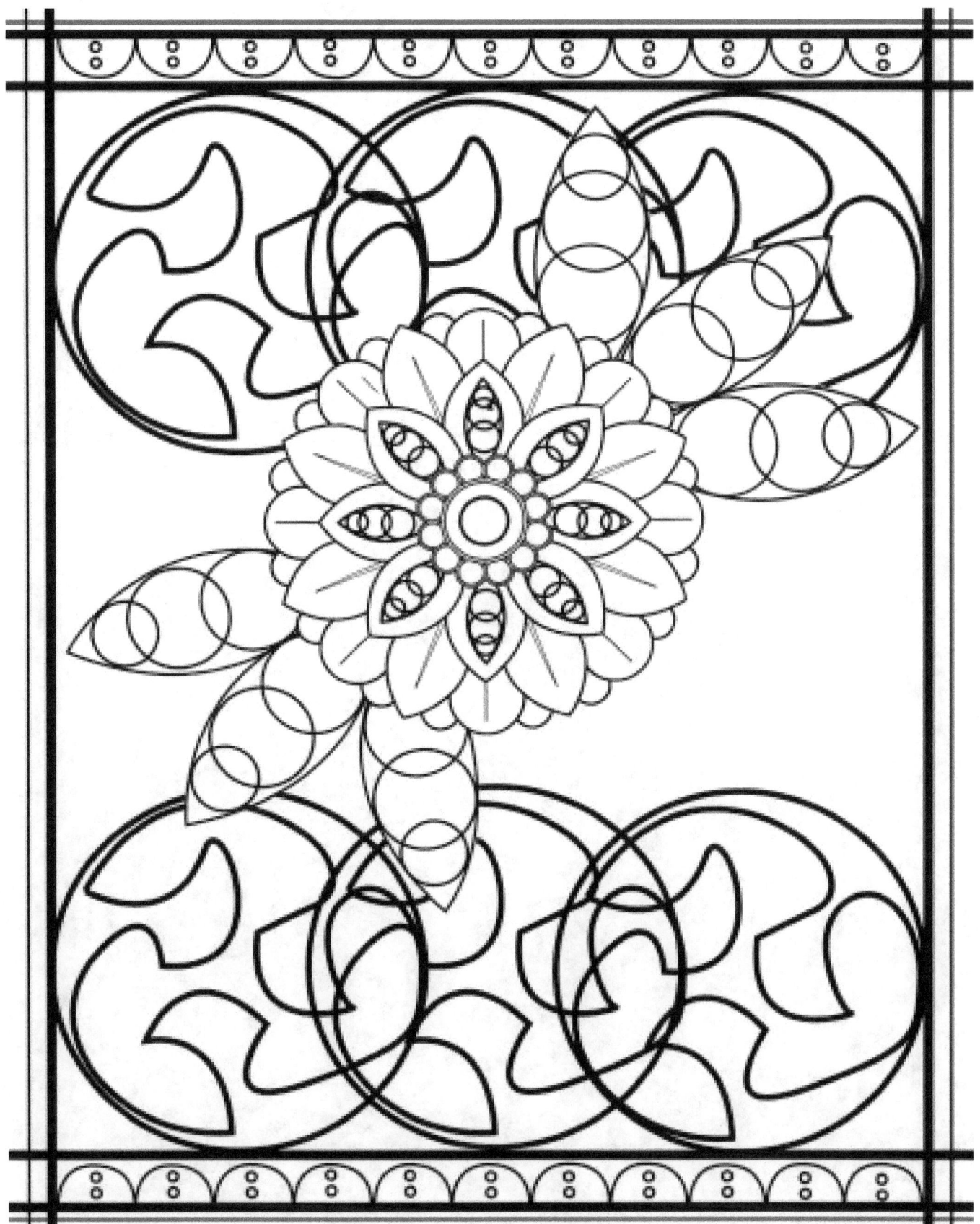

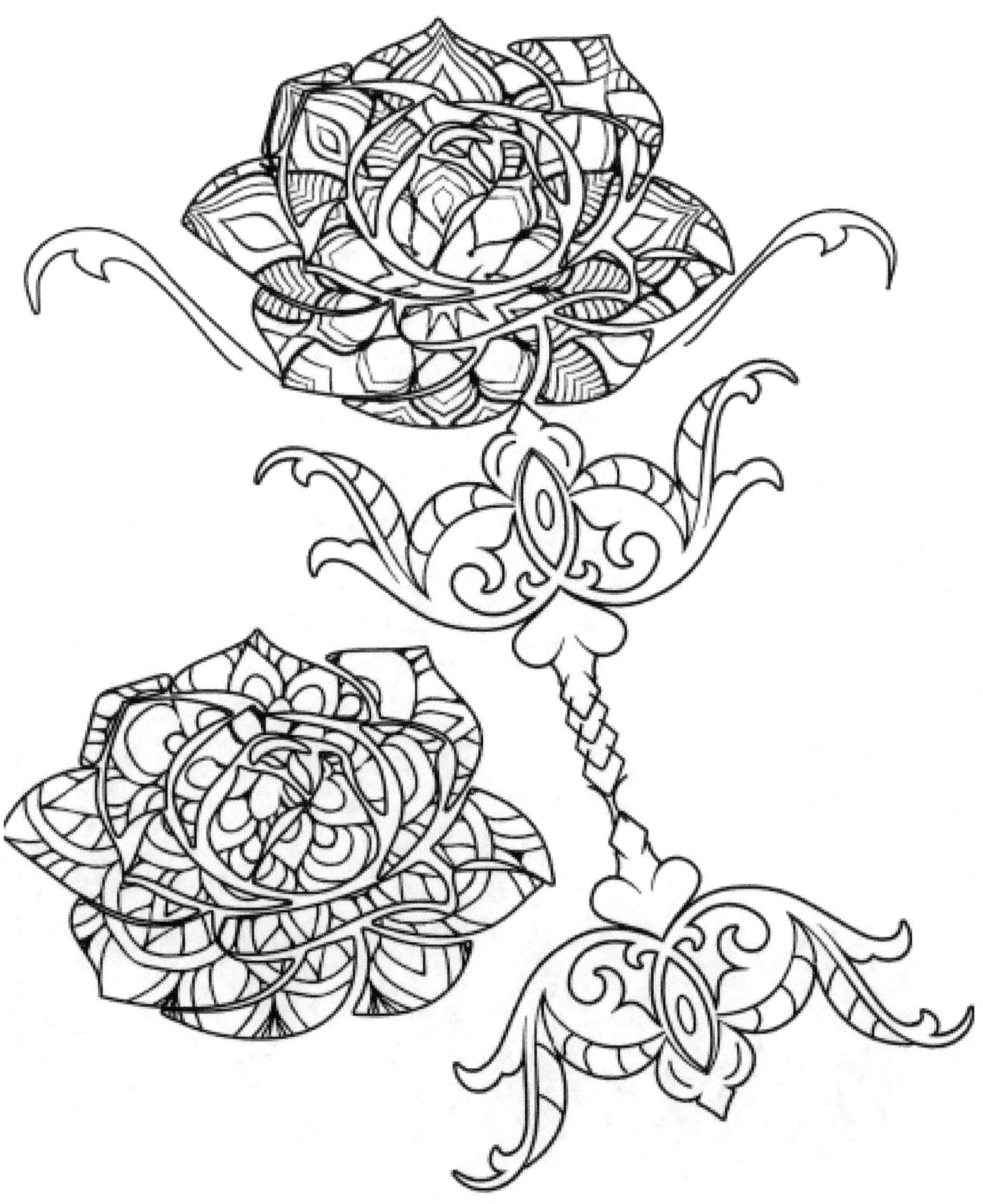

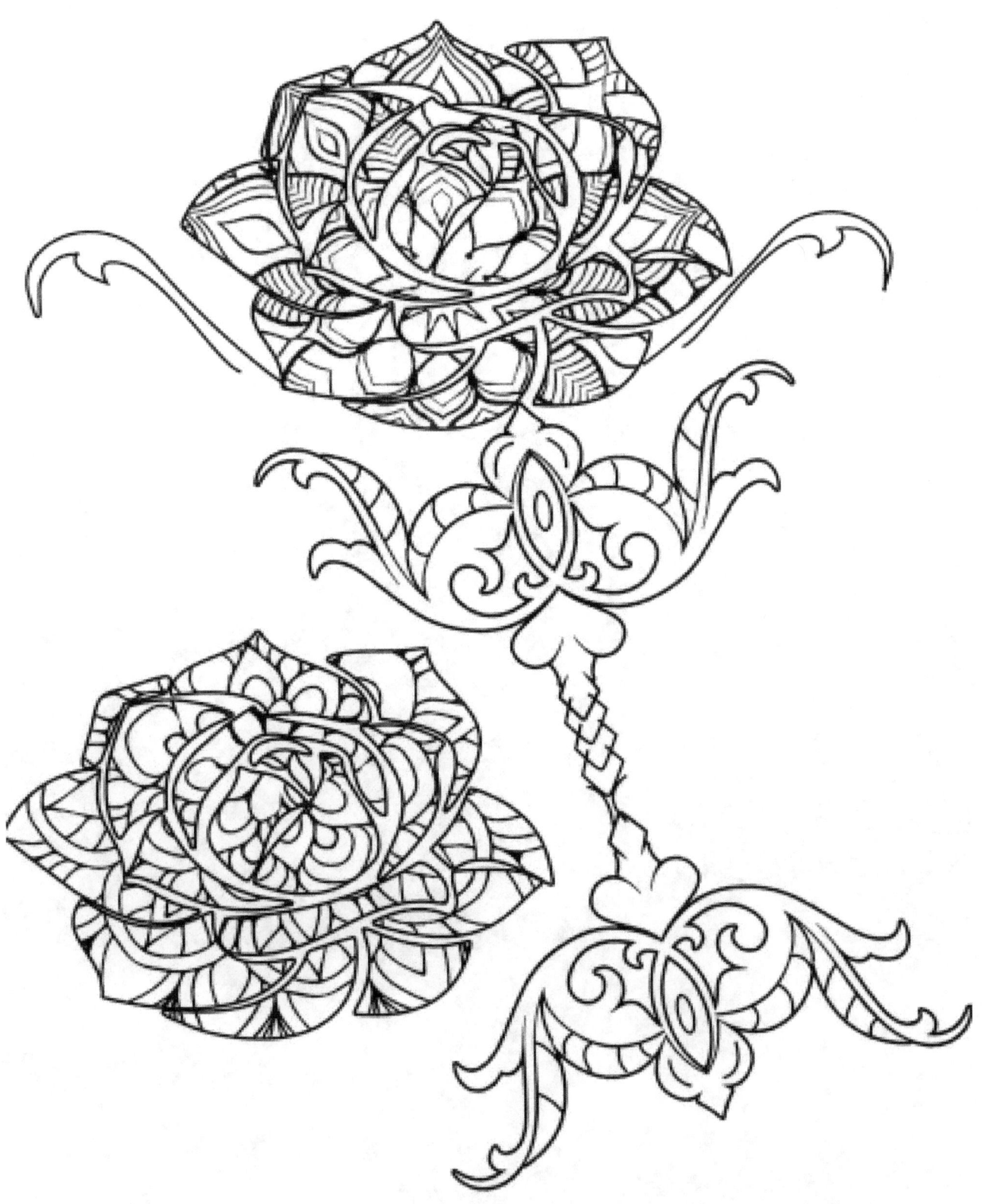

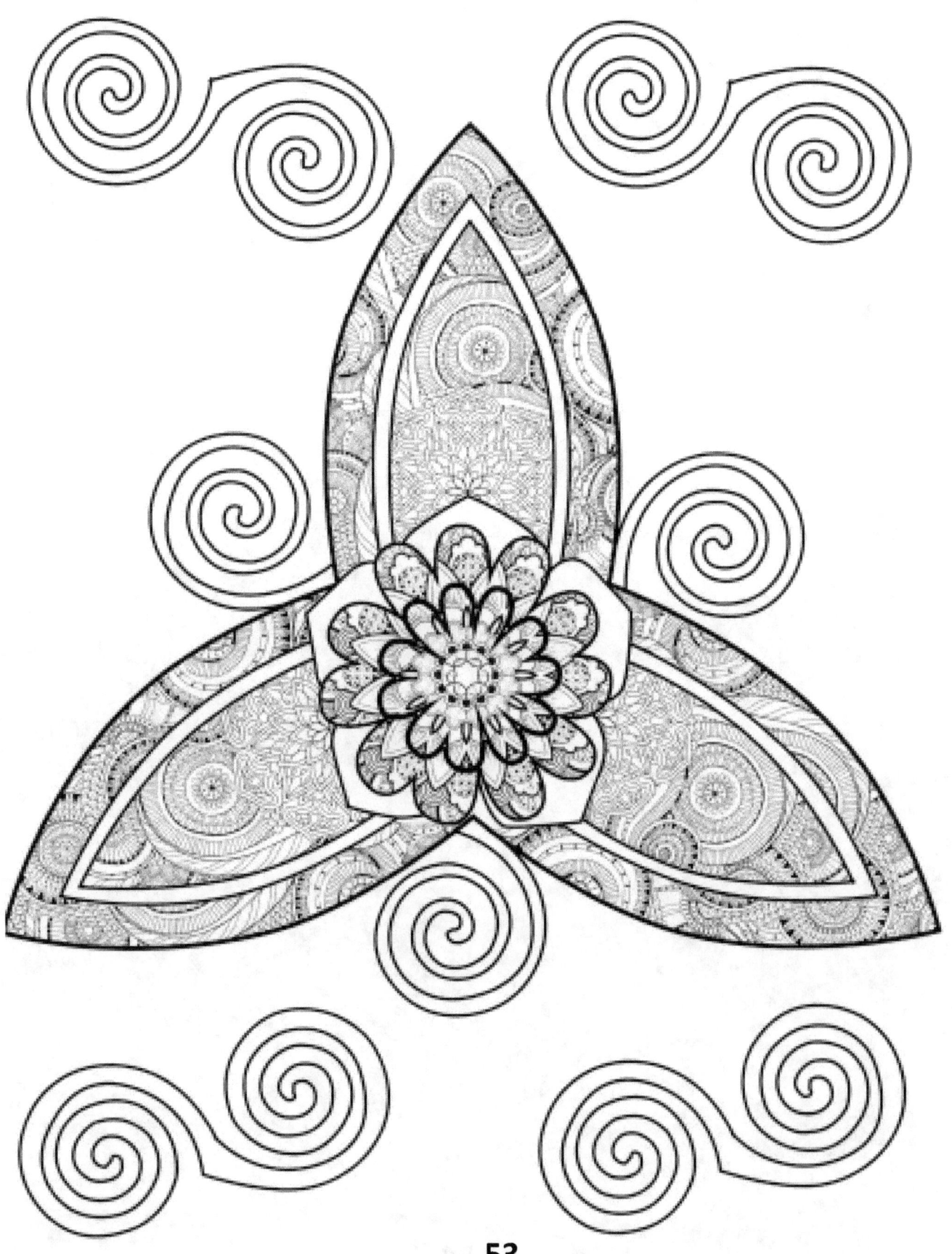

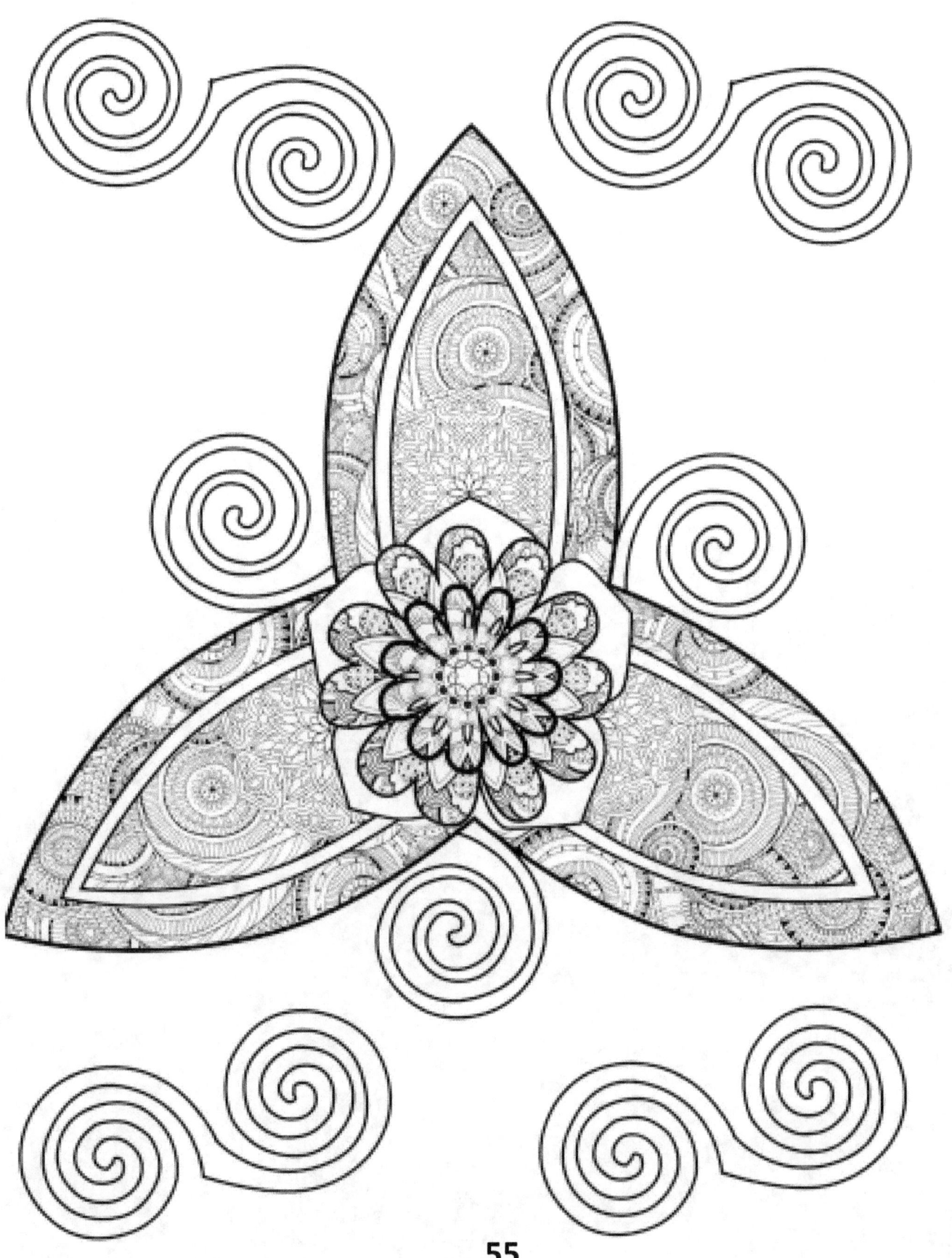

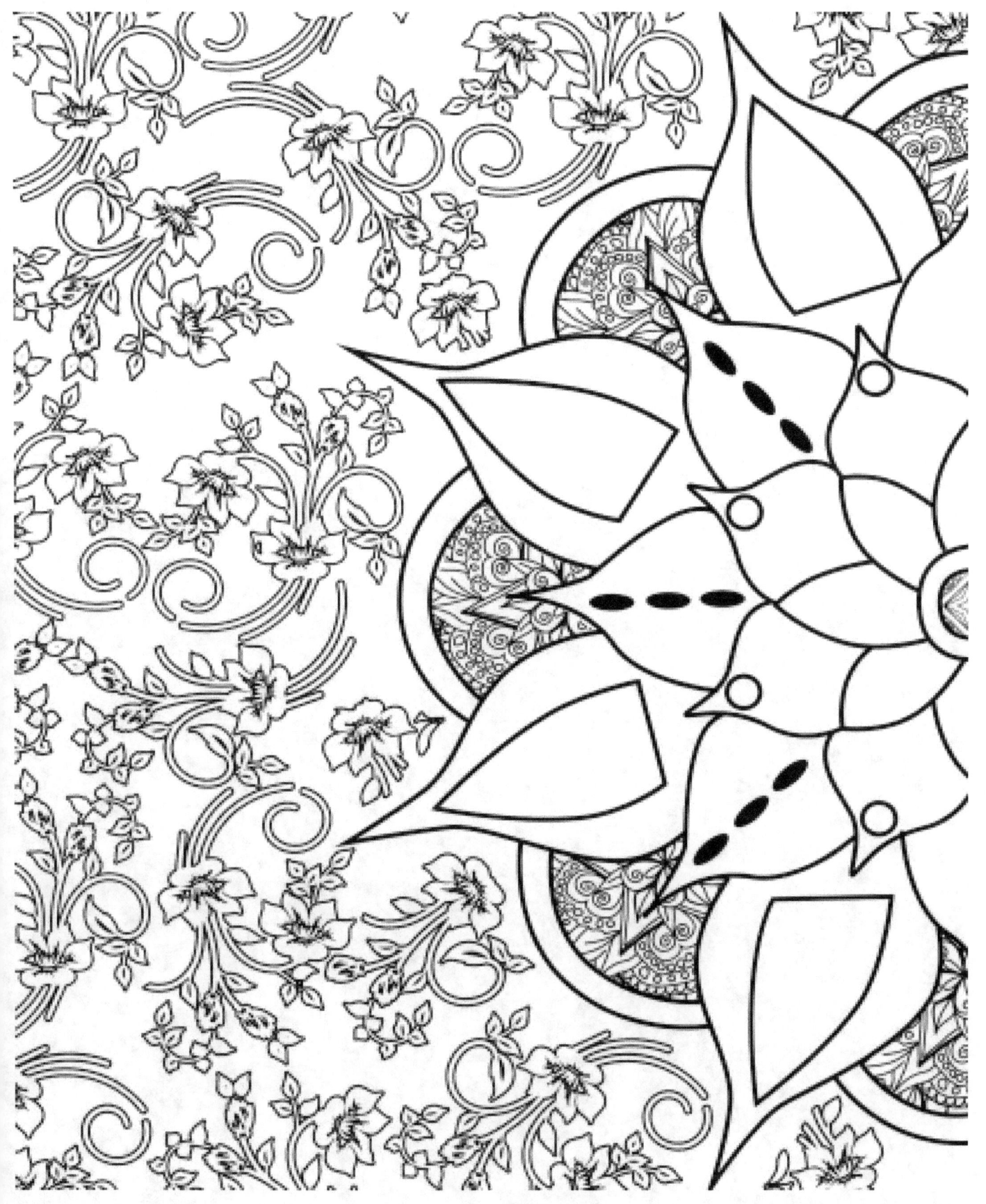

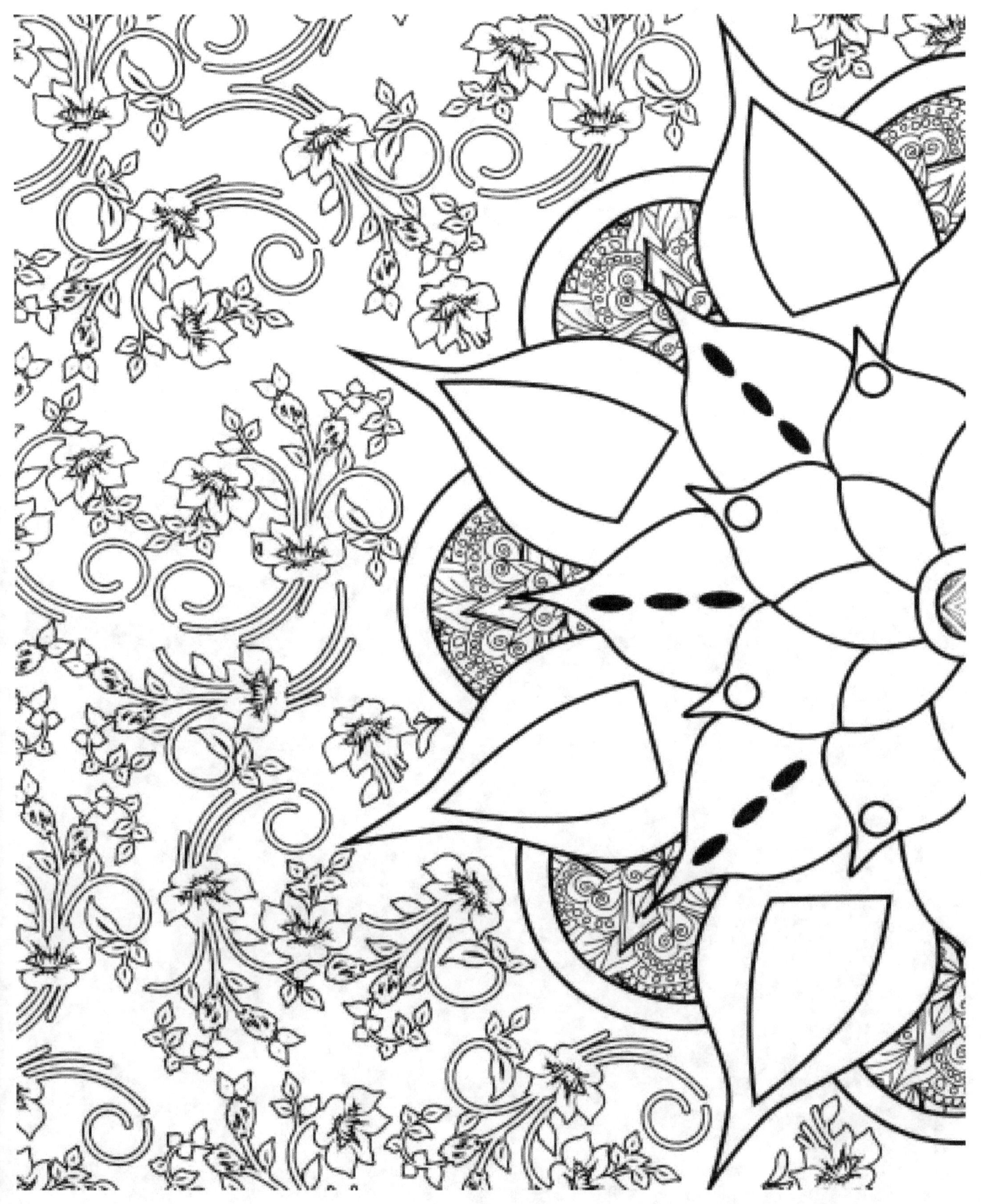

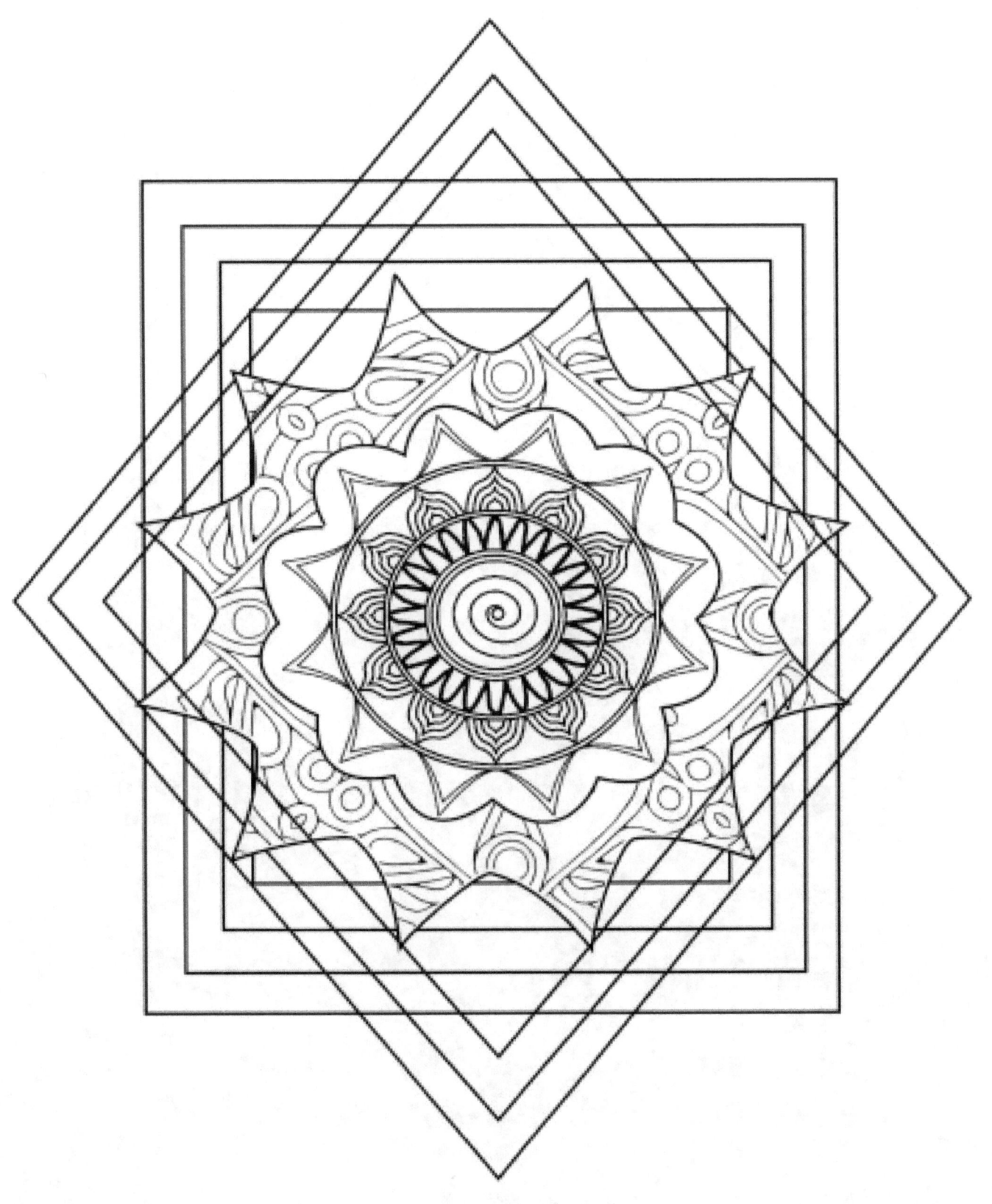

61

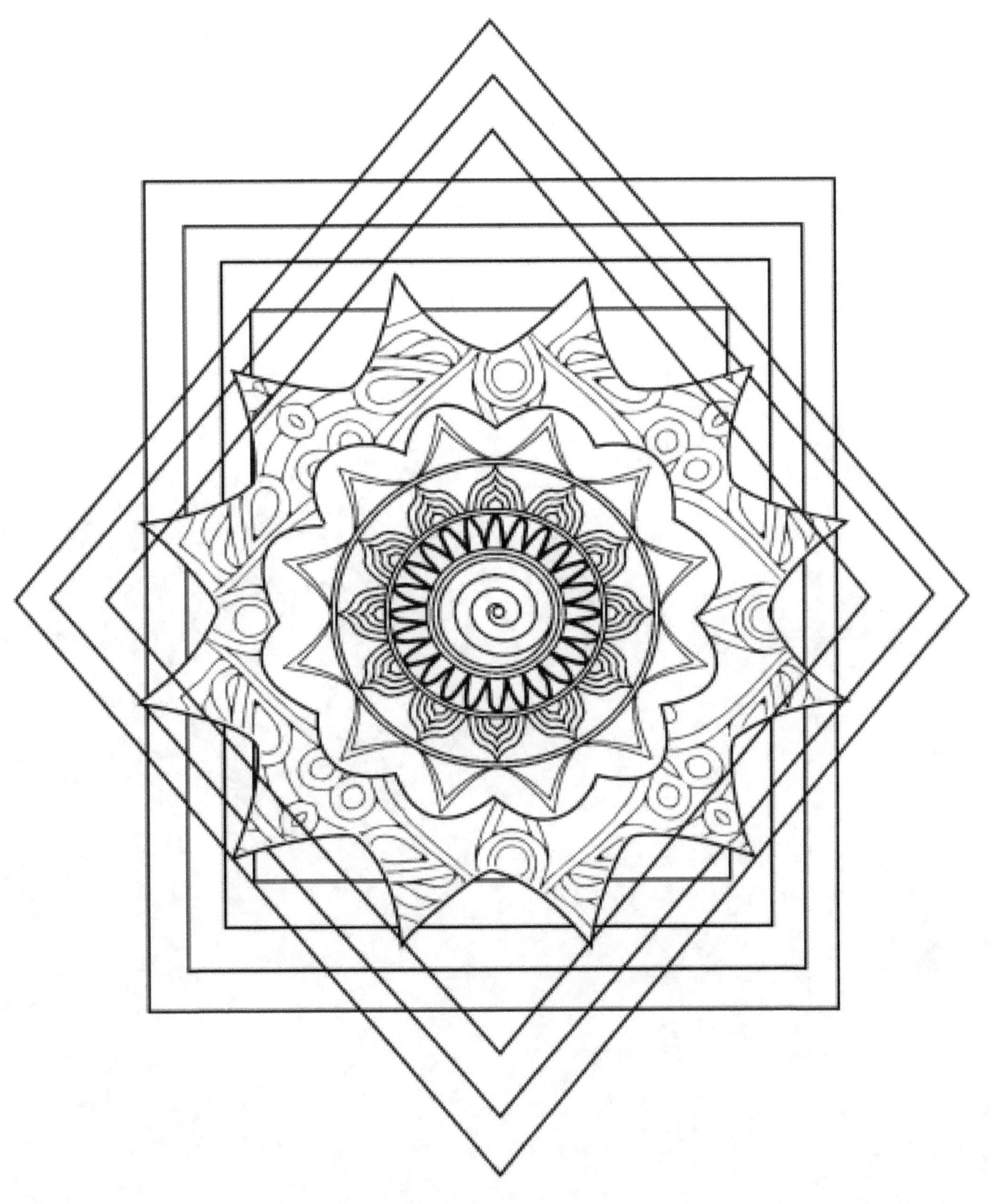

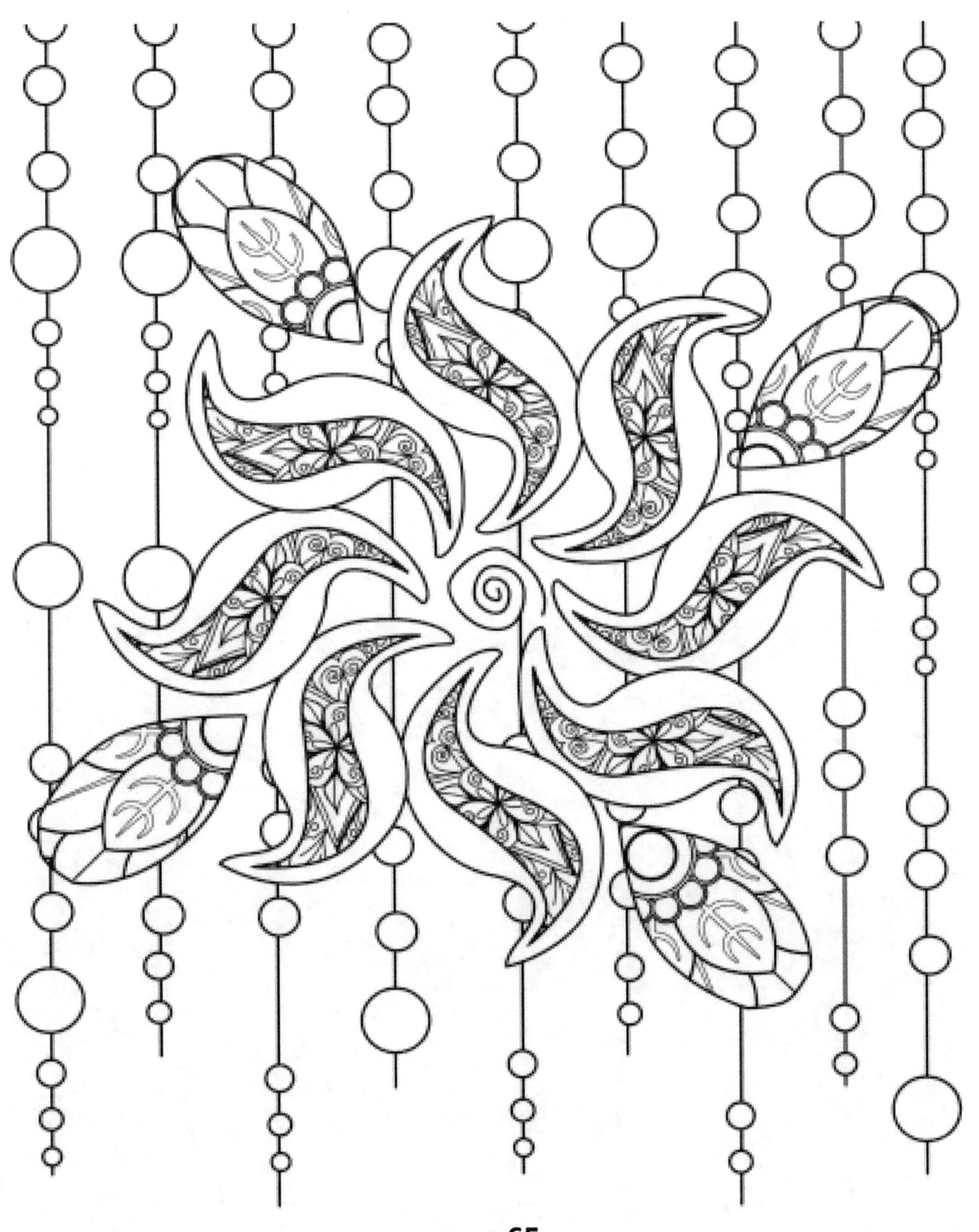

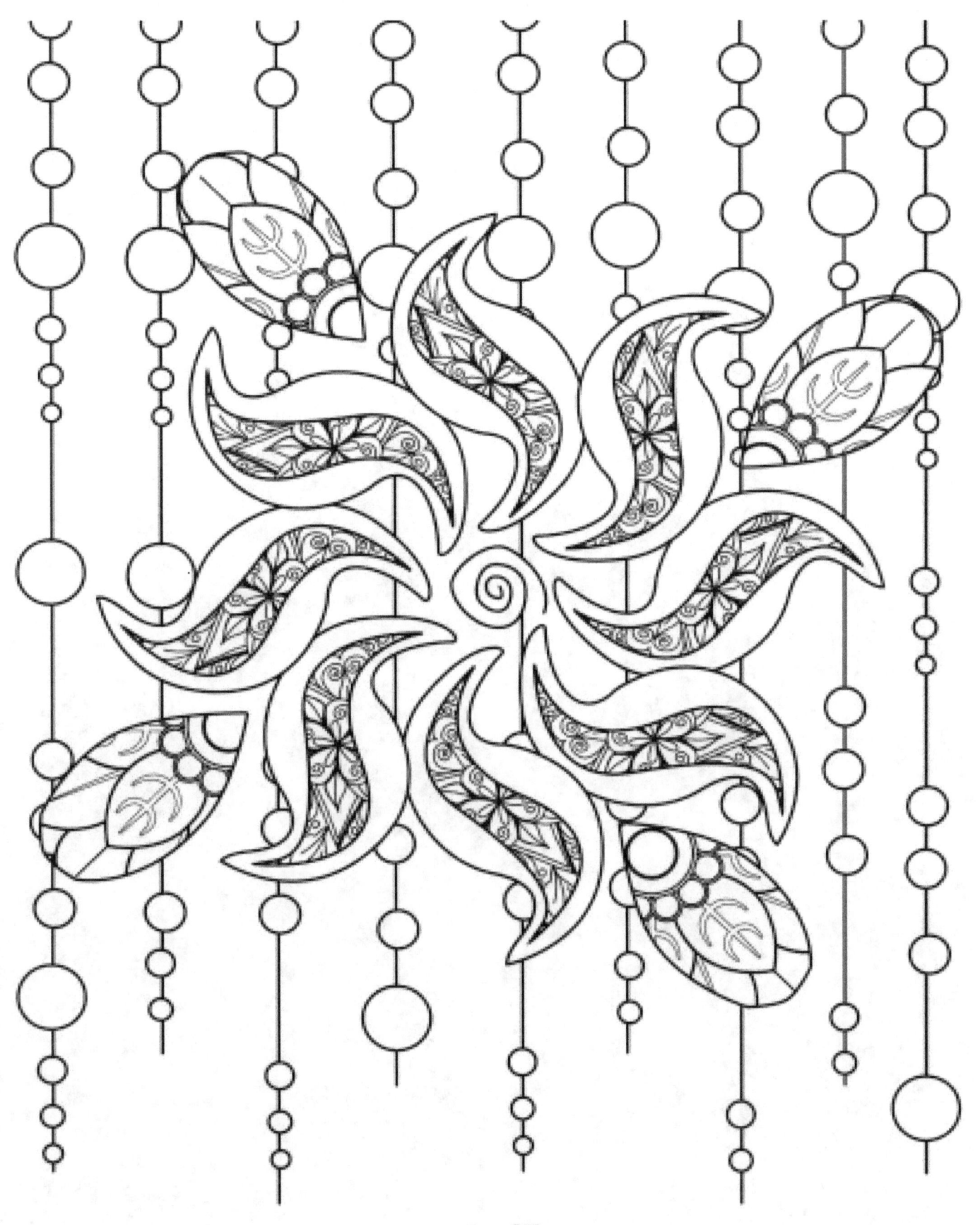

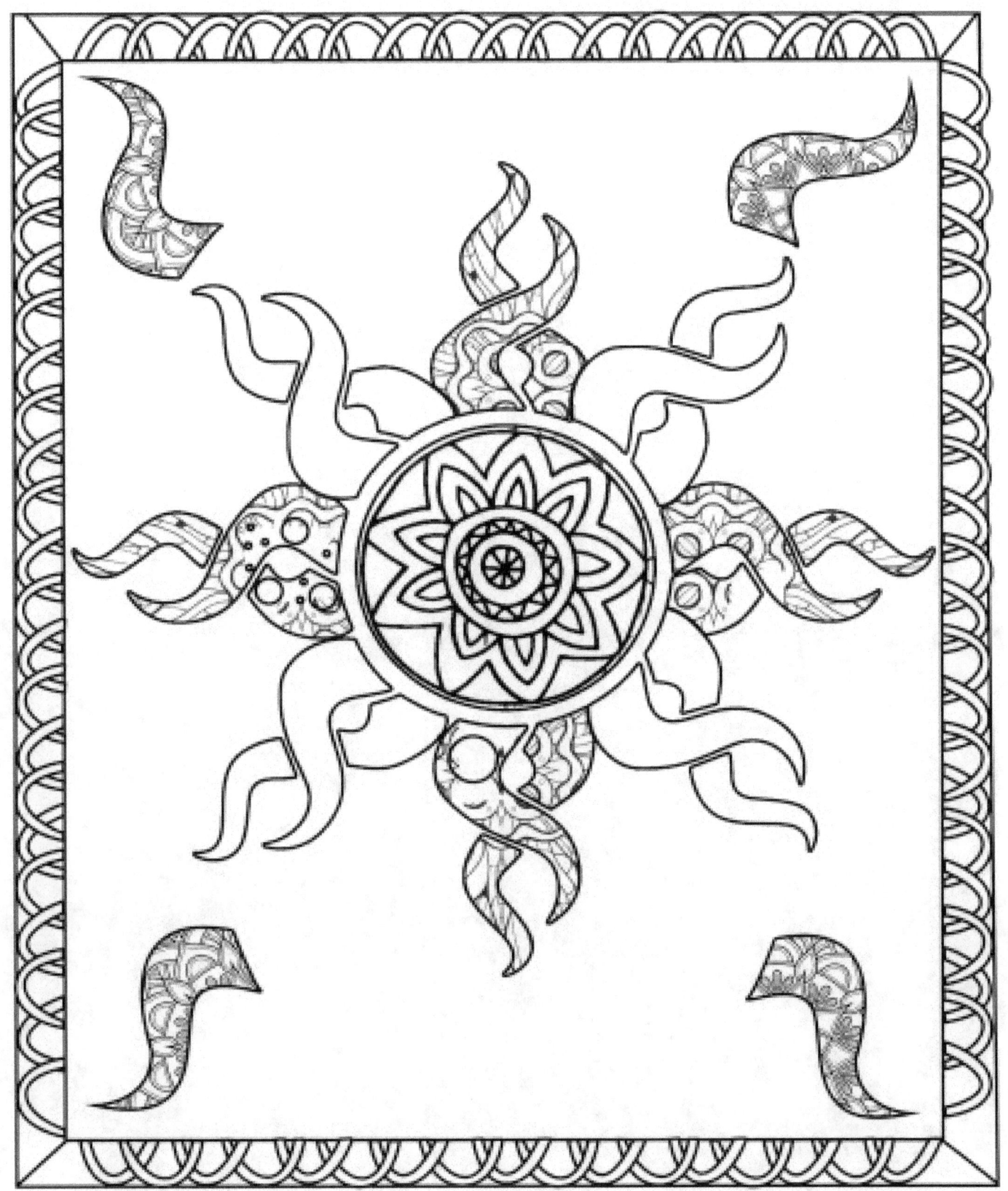

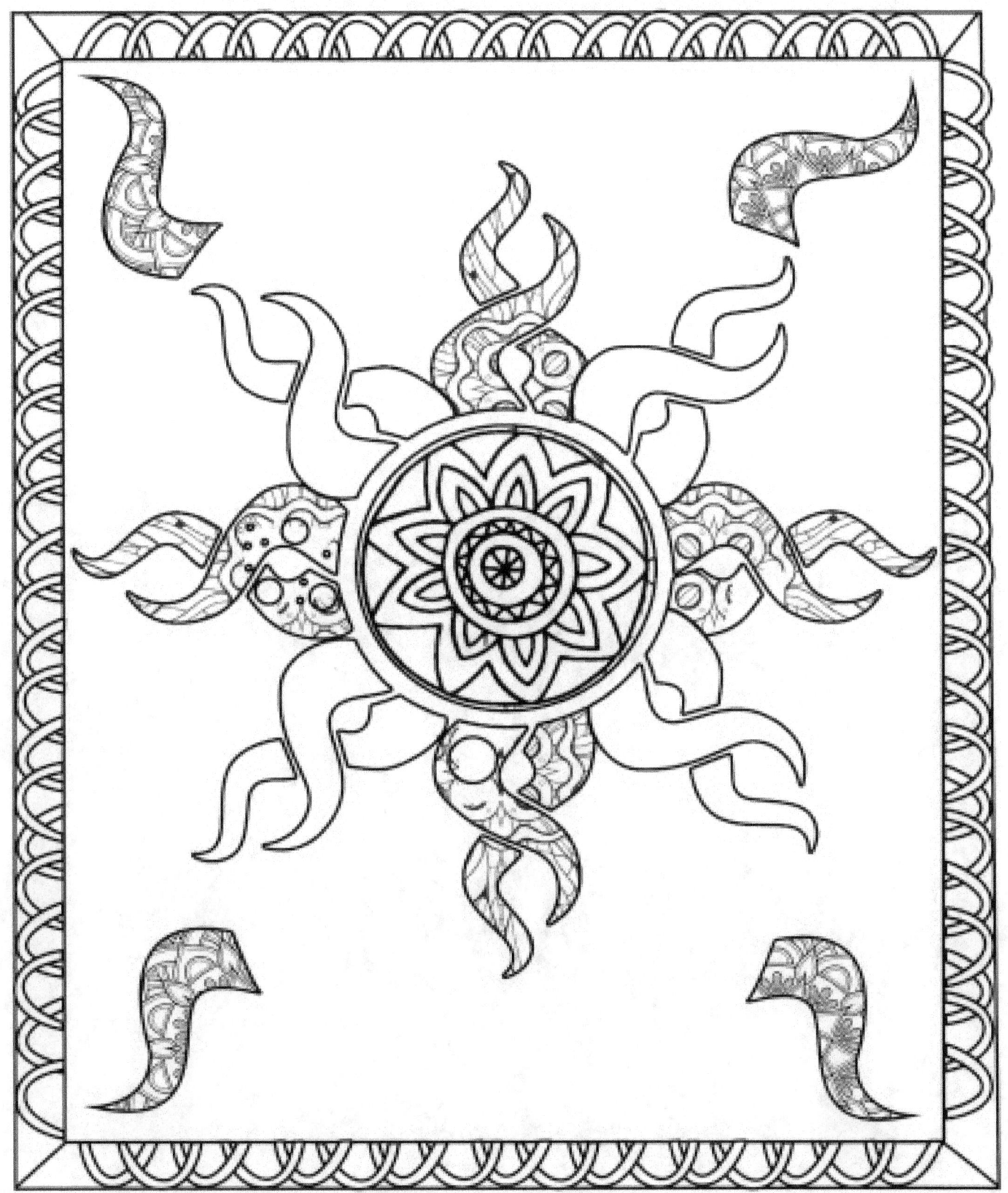

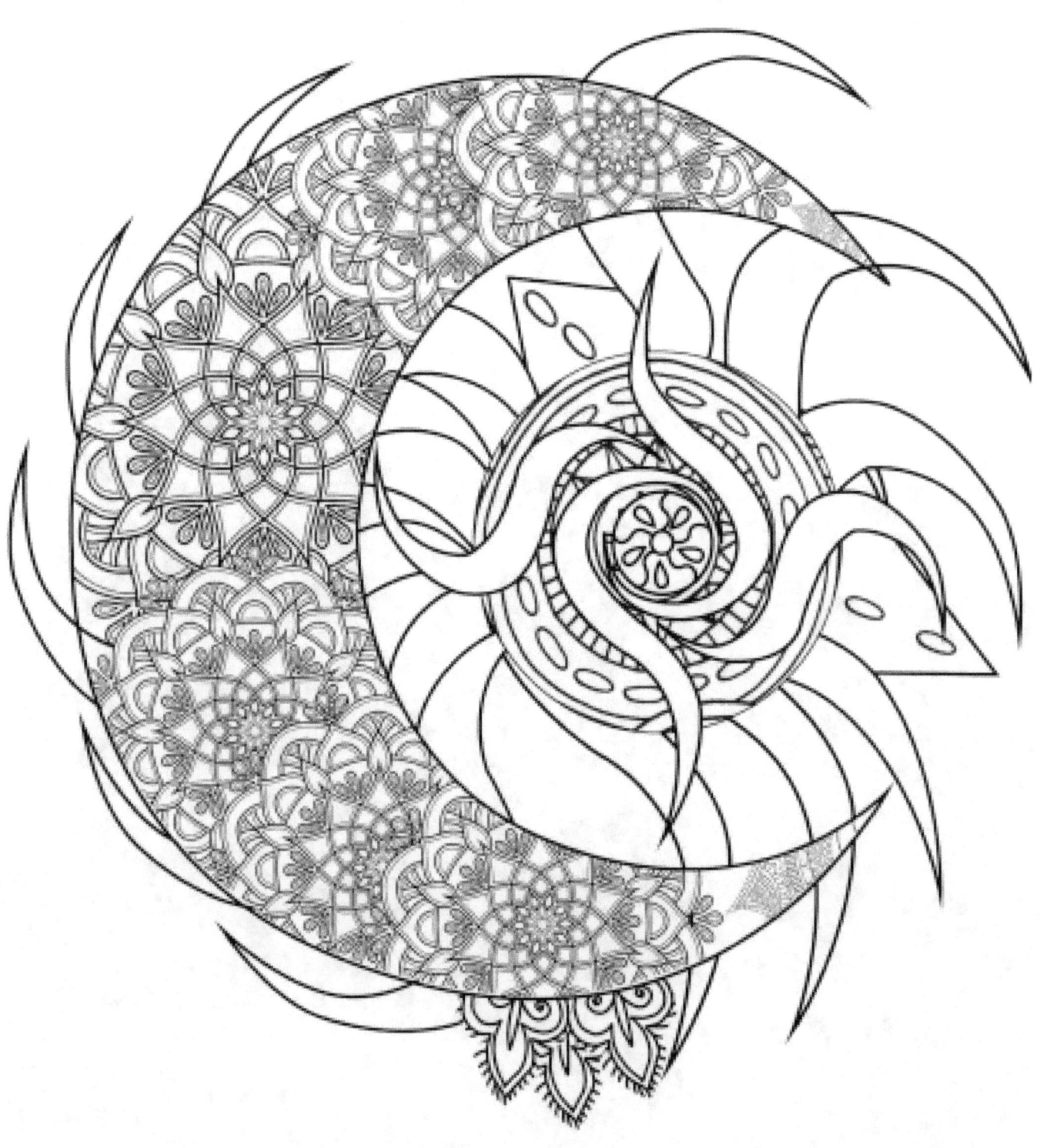

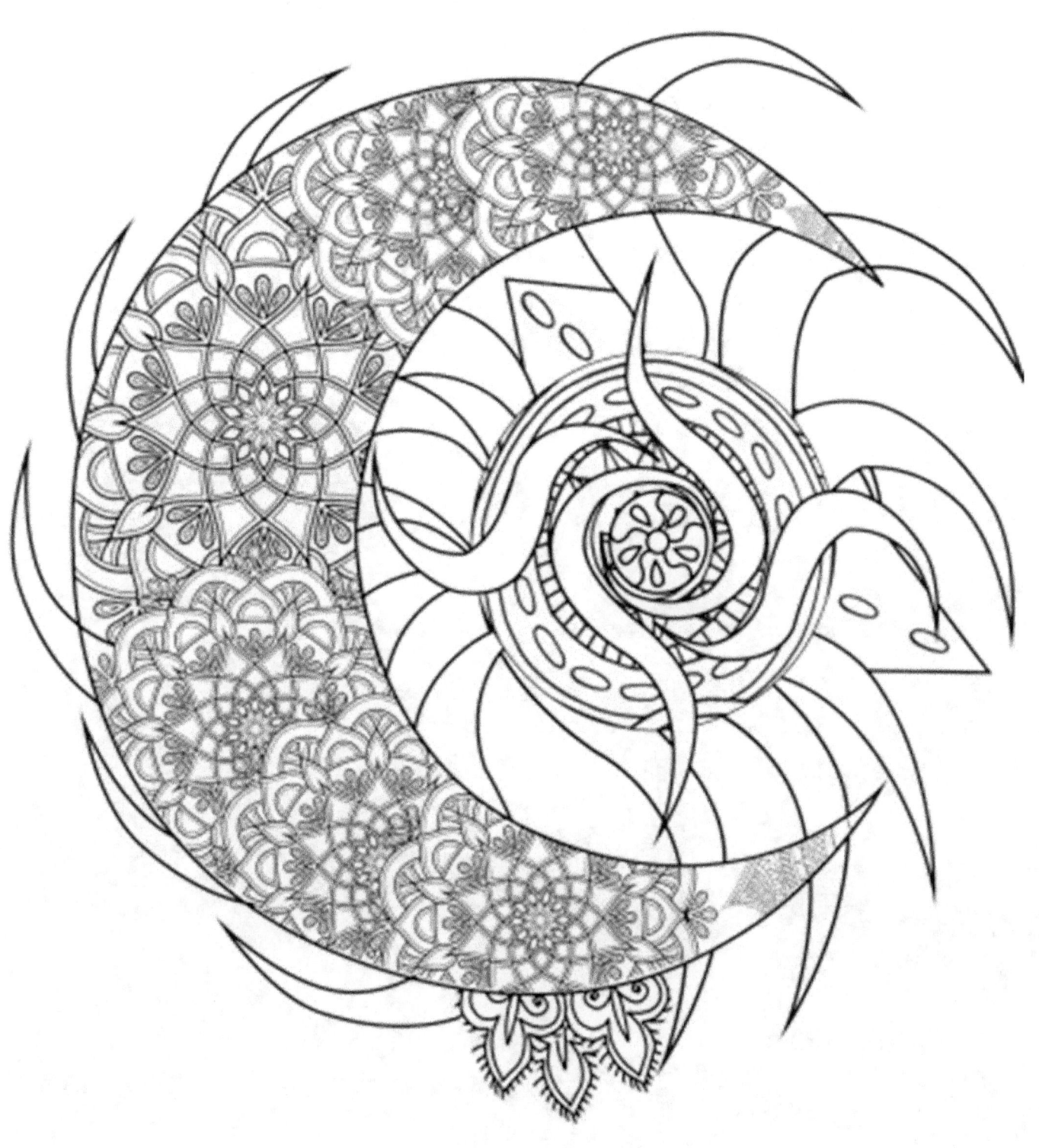

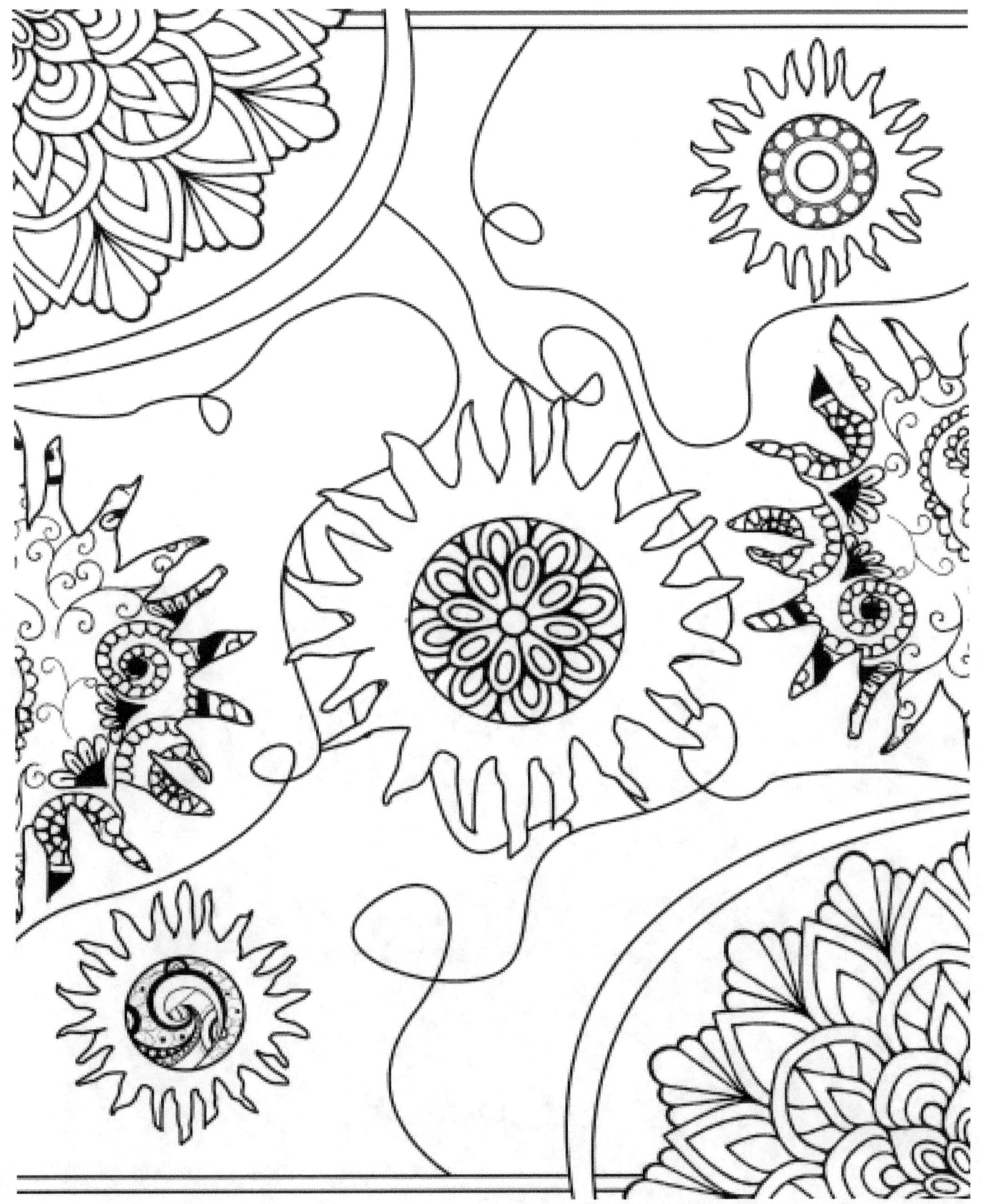

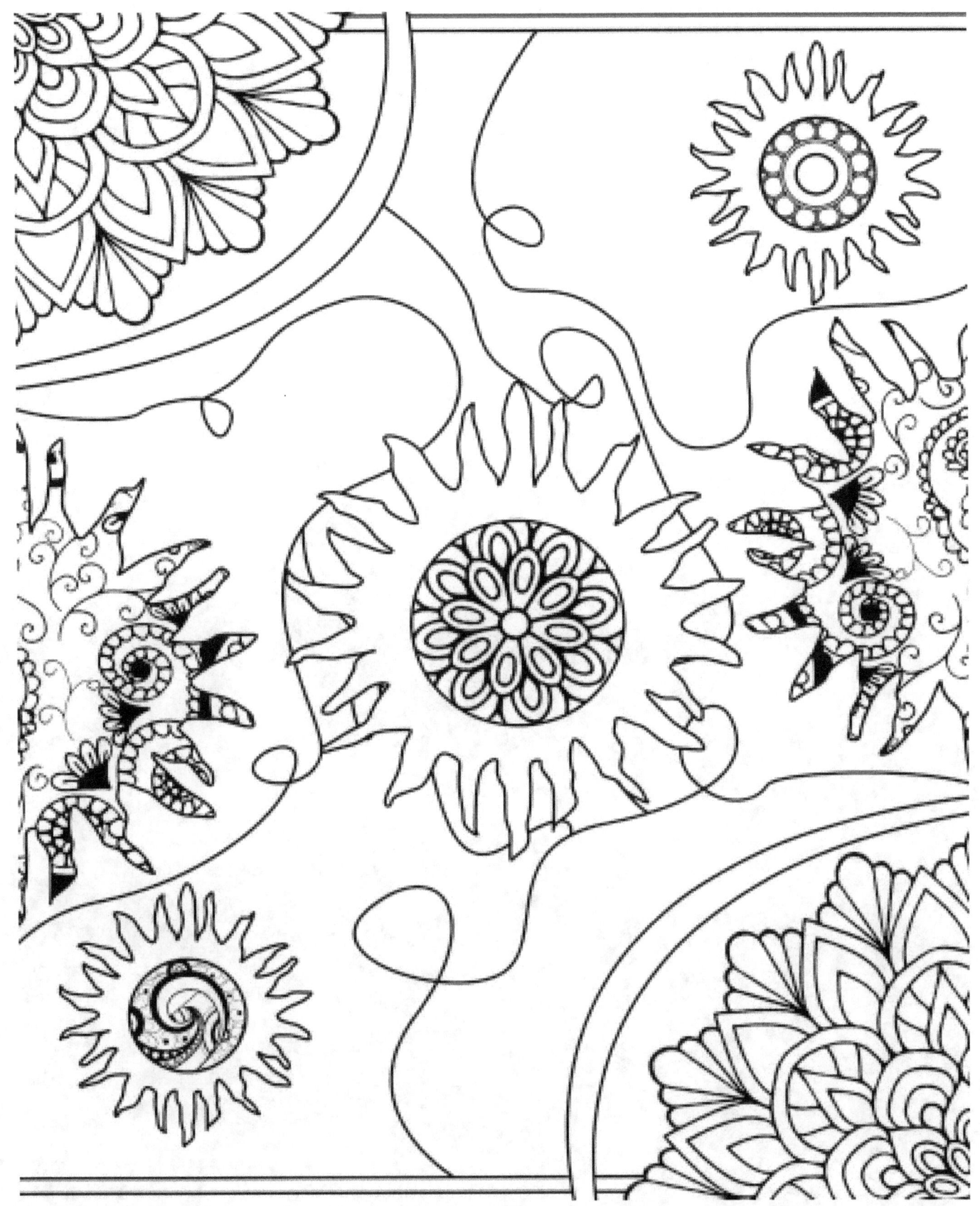

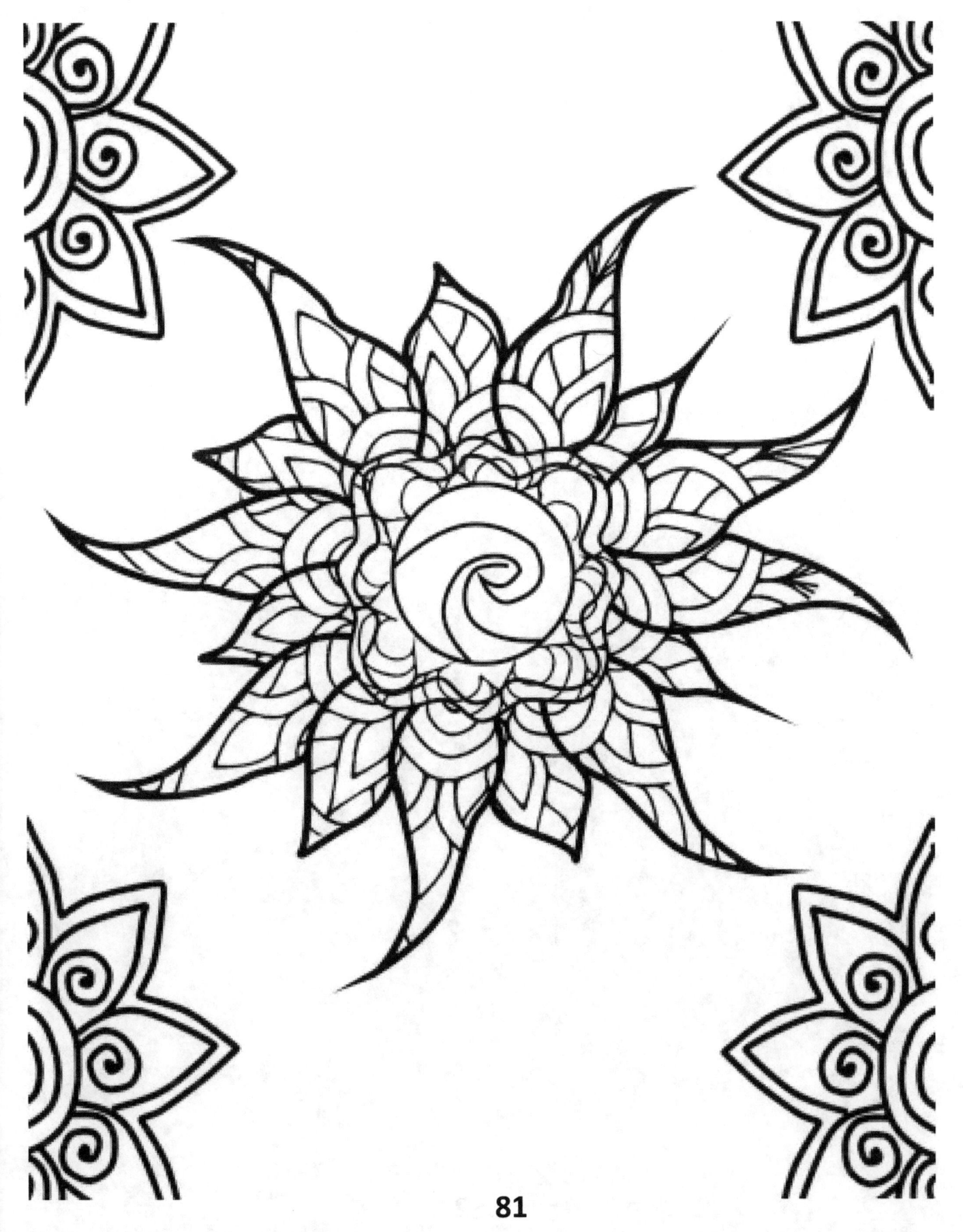

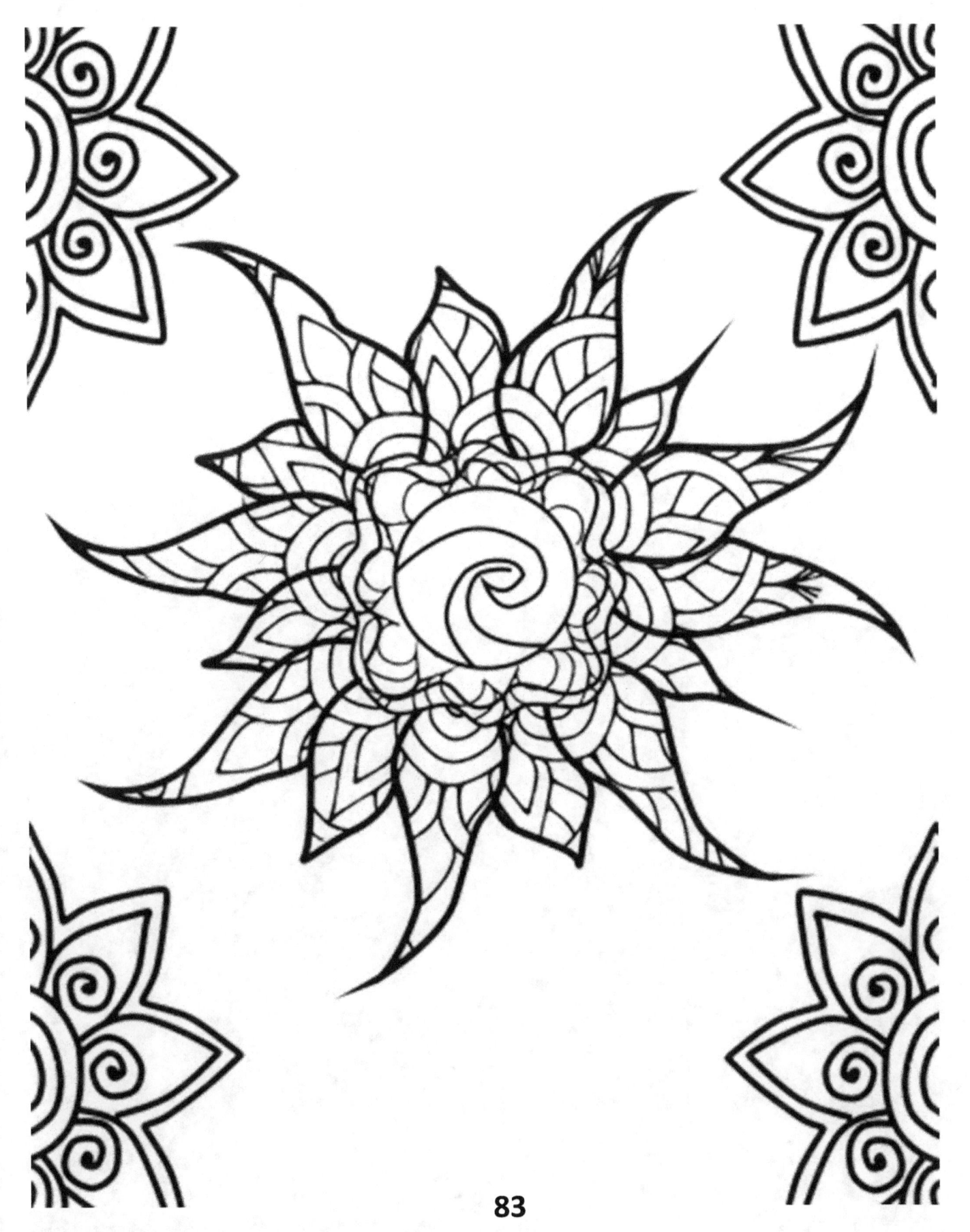

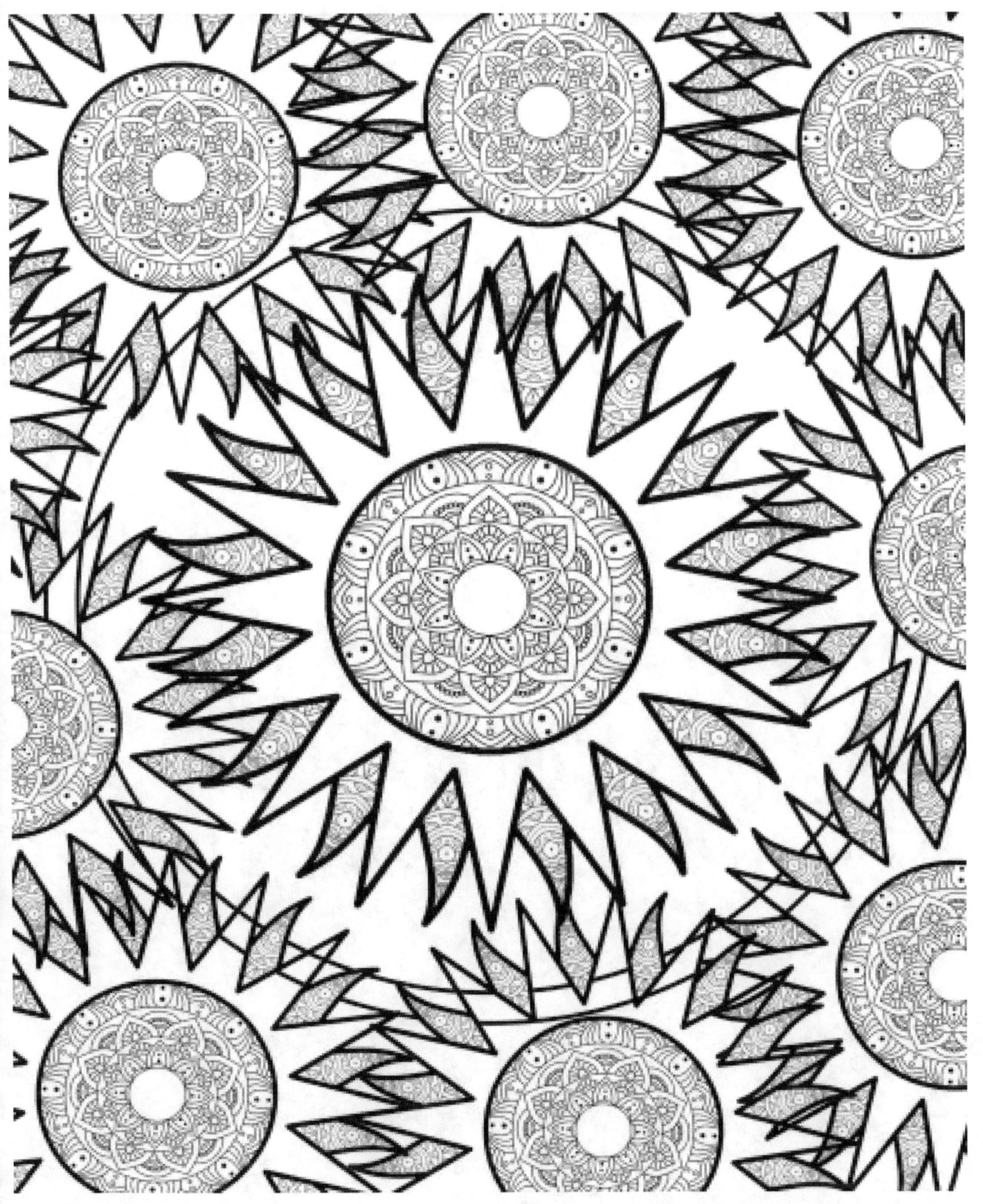

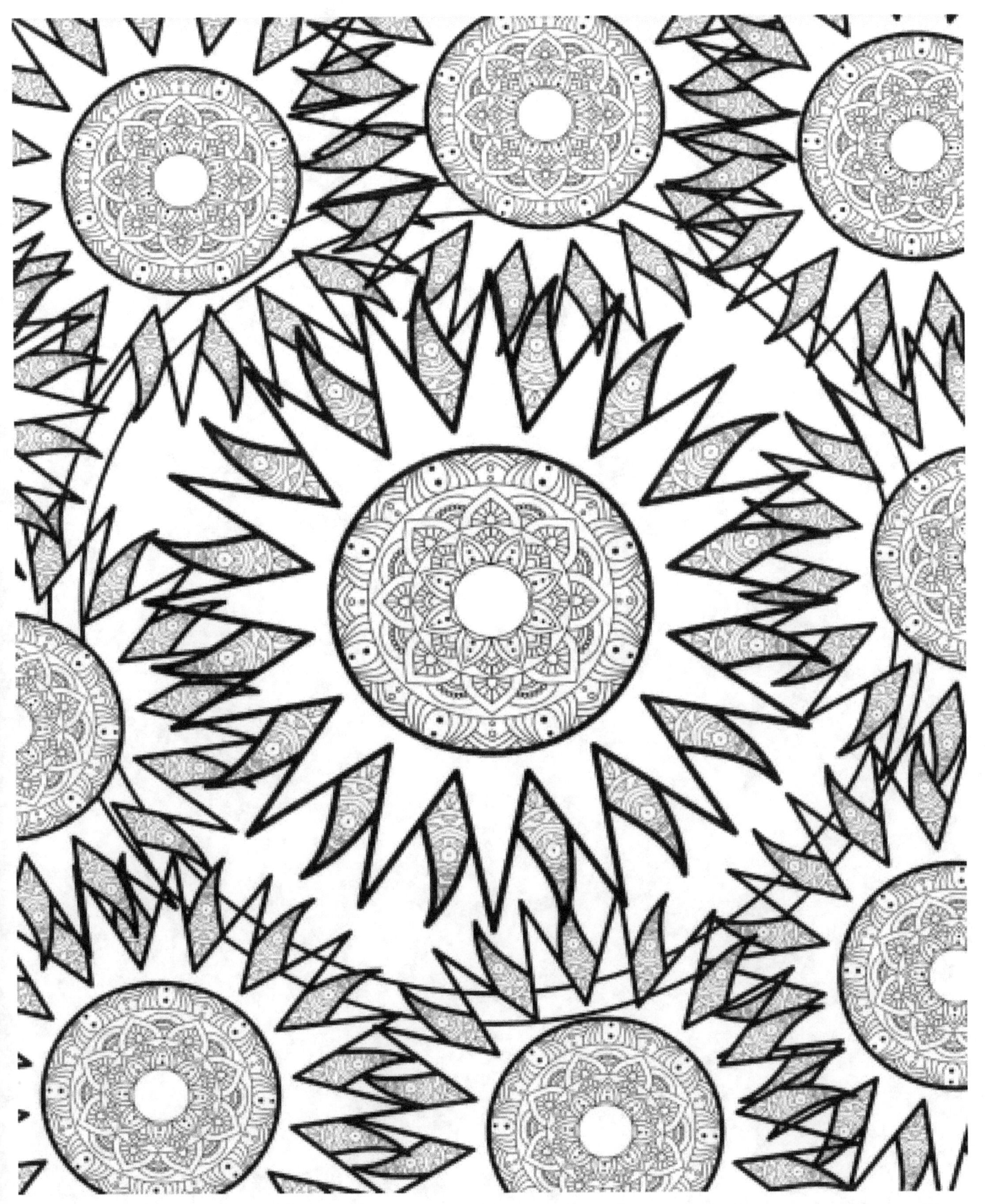

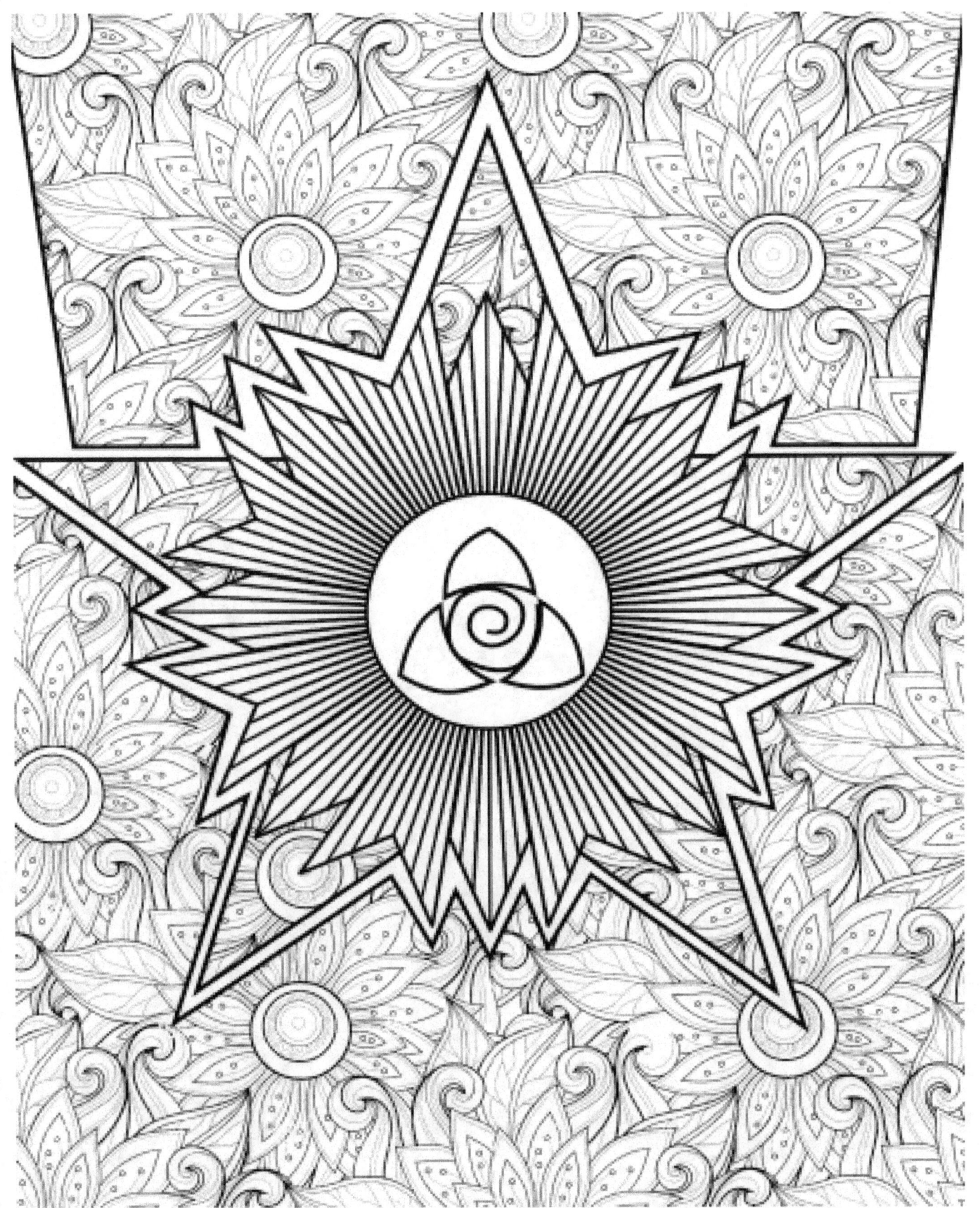

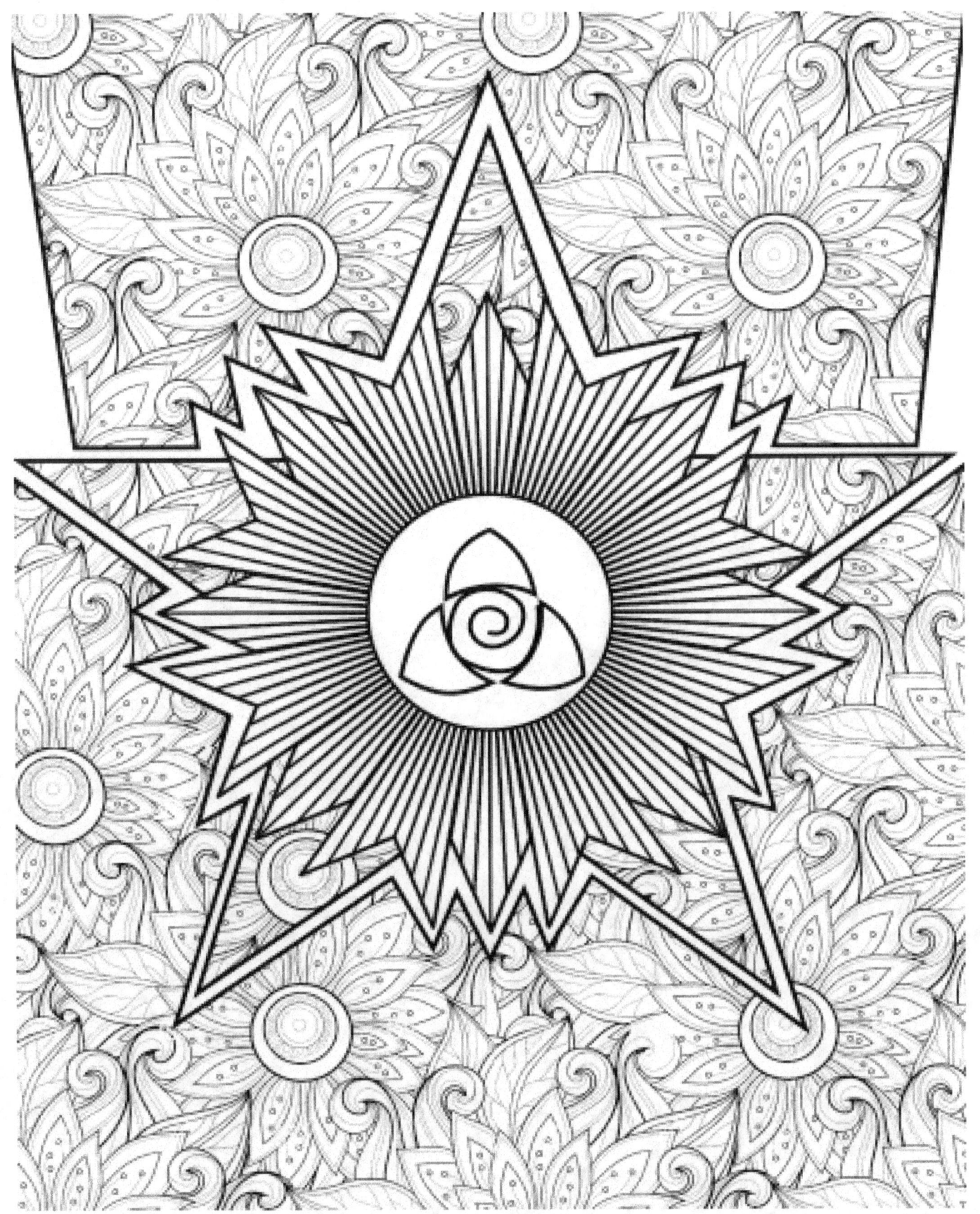

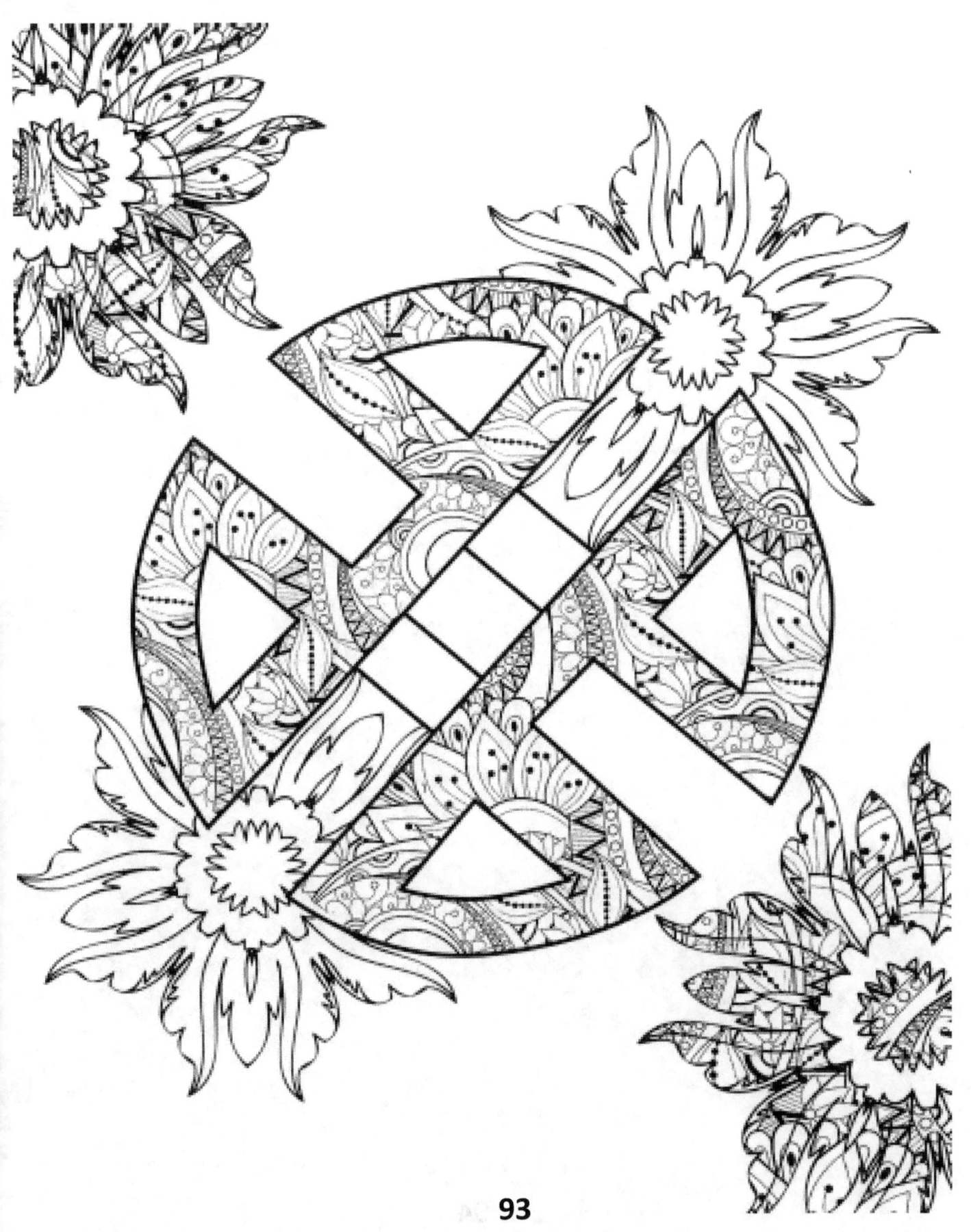

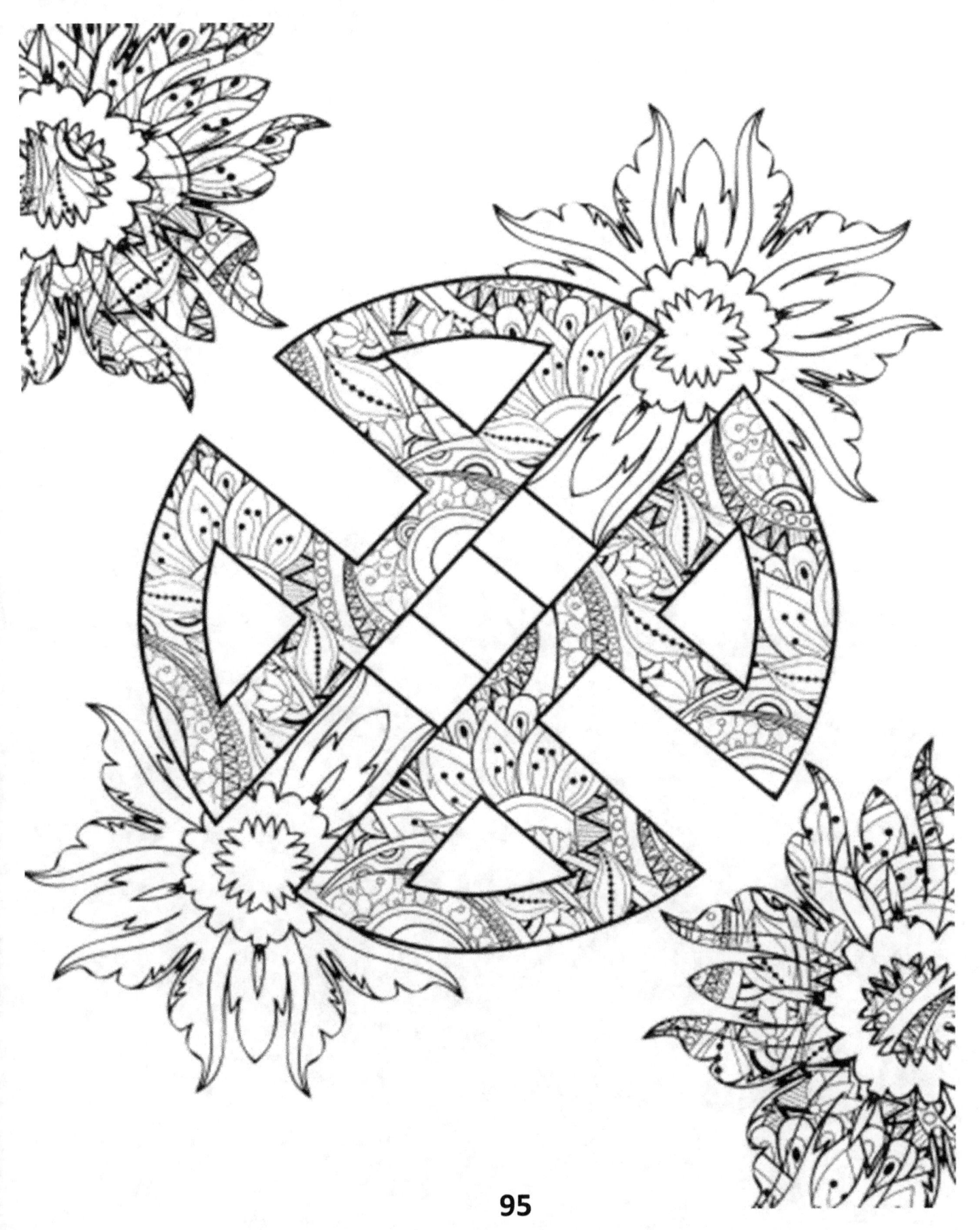

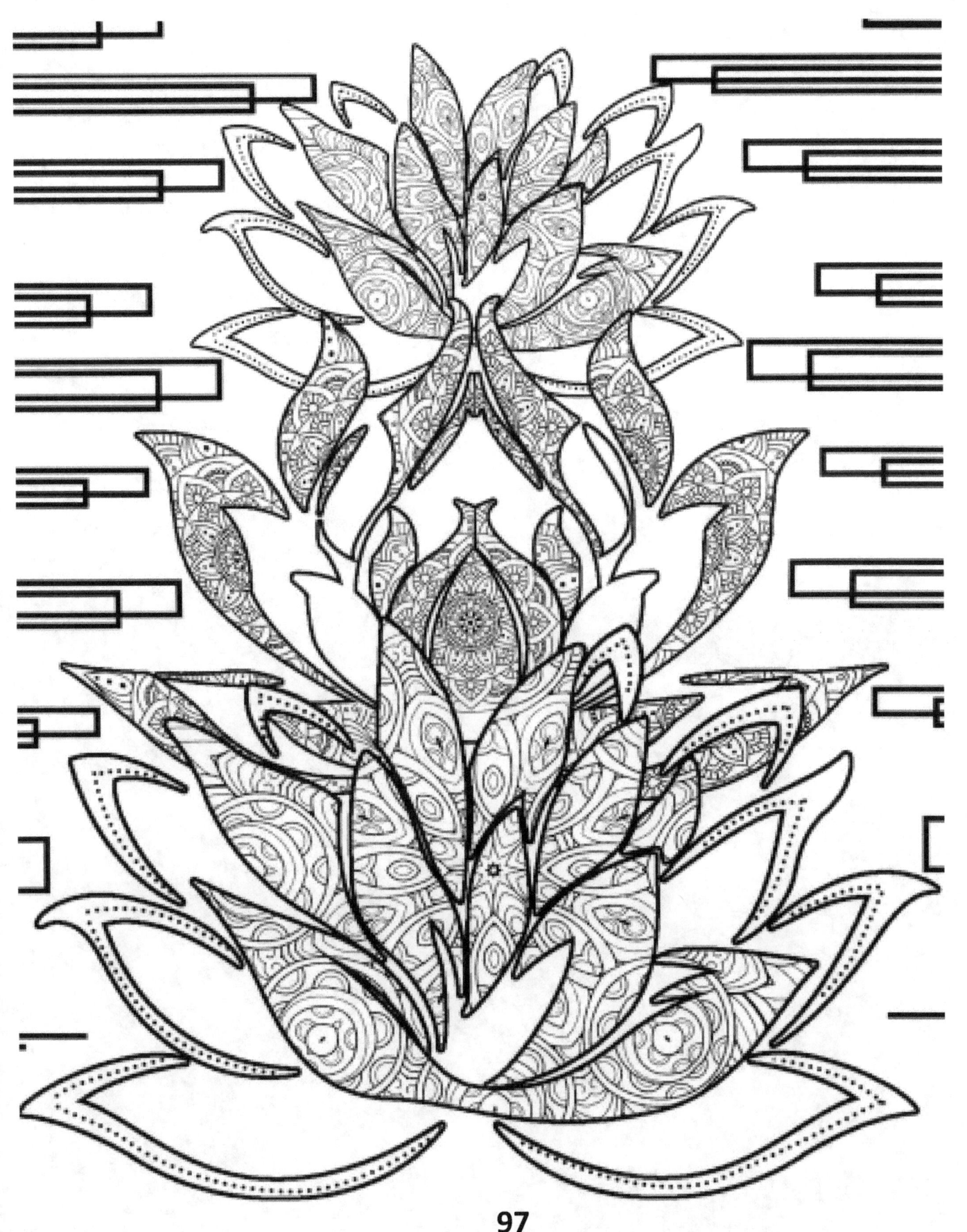

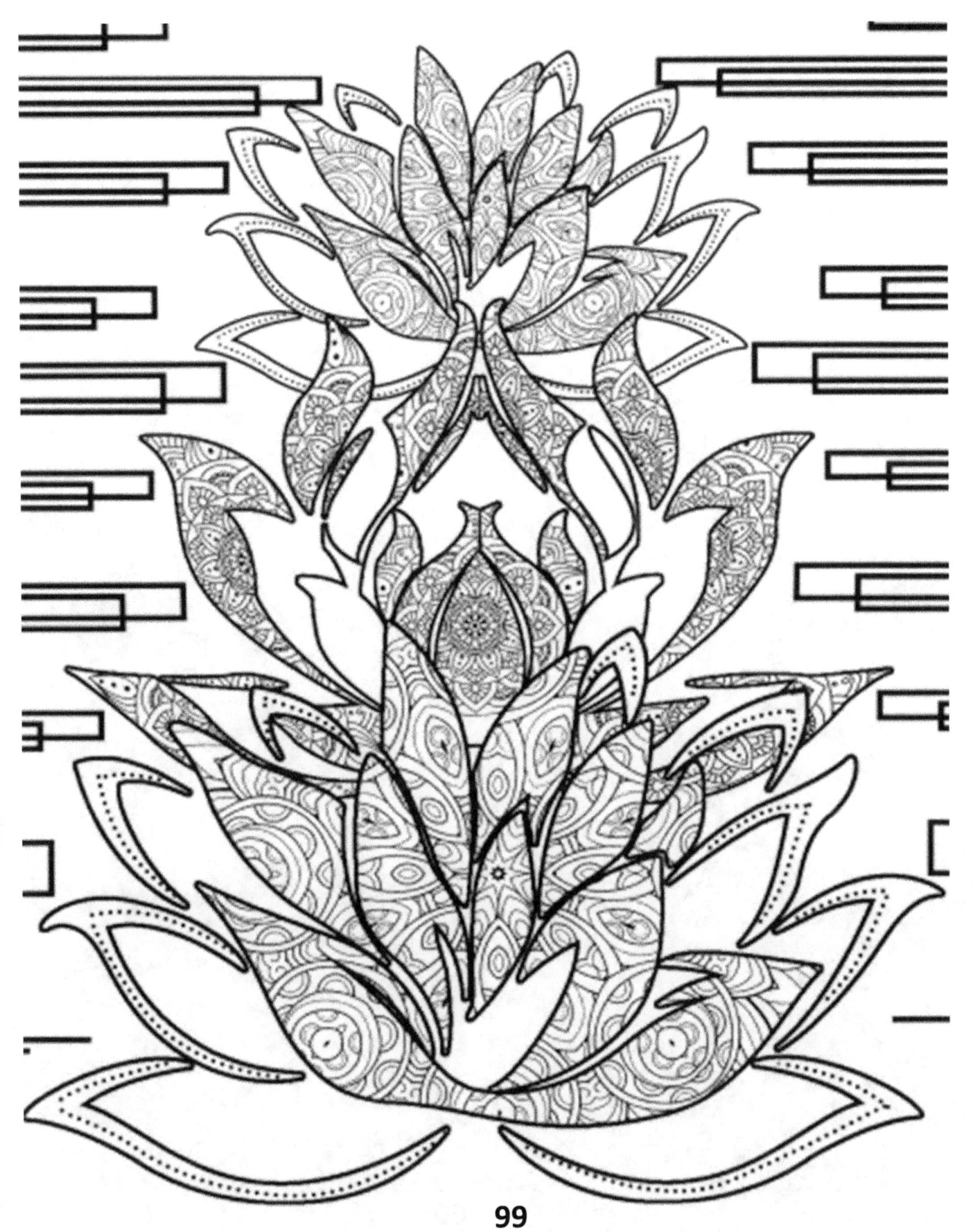

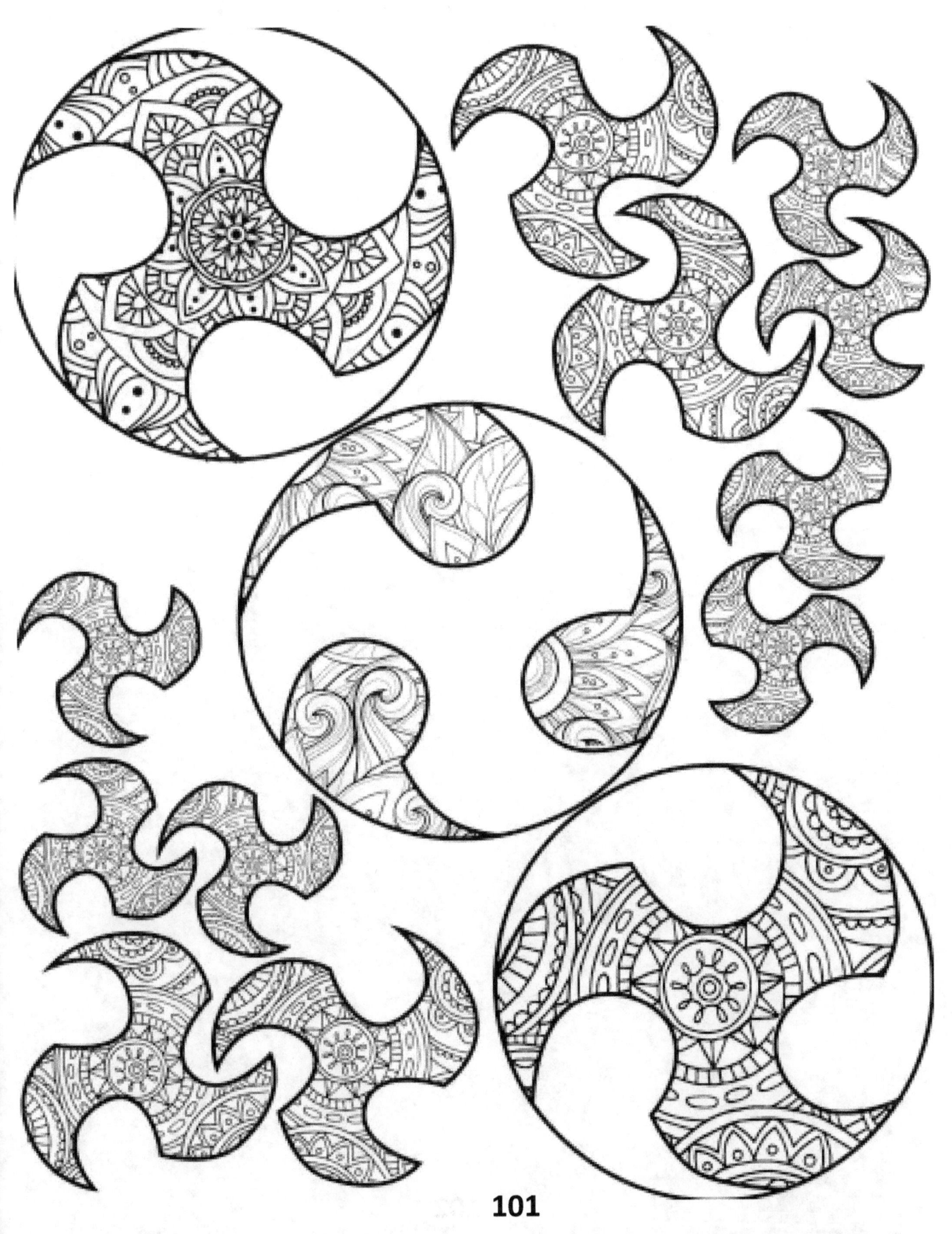

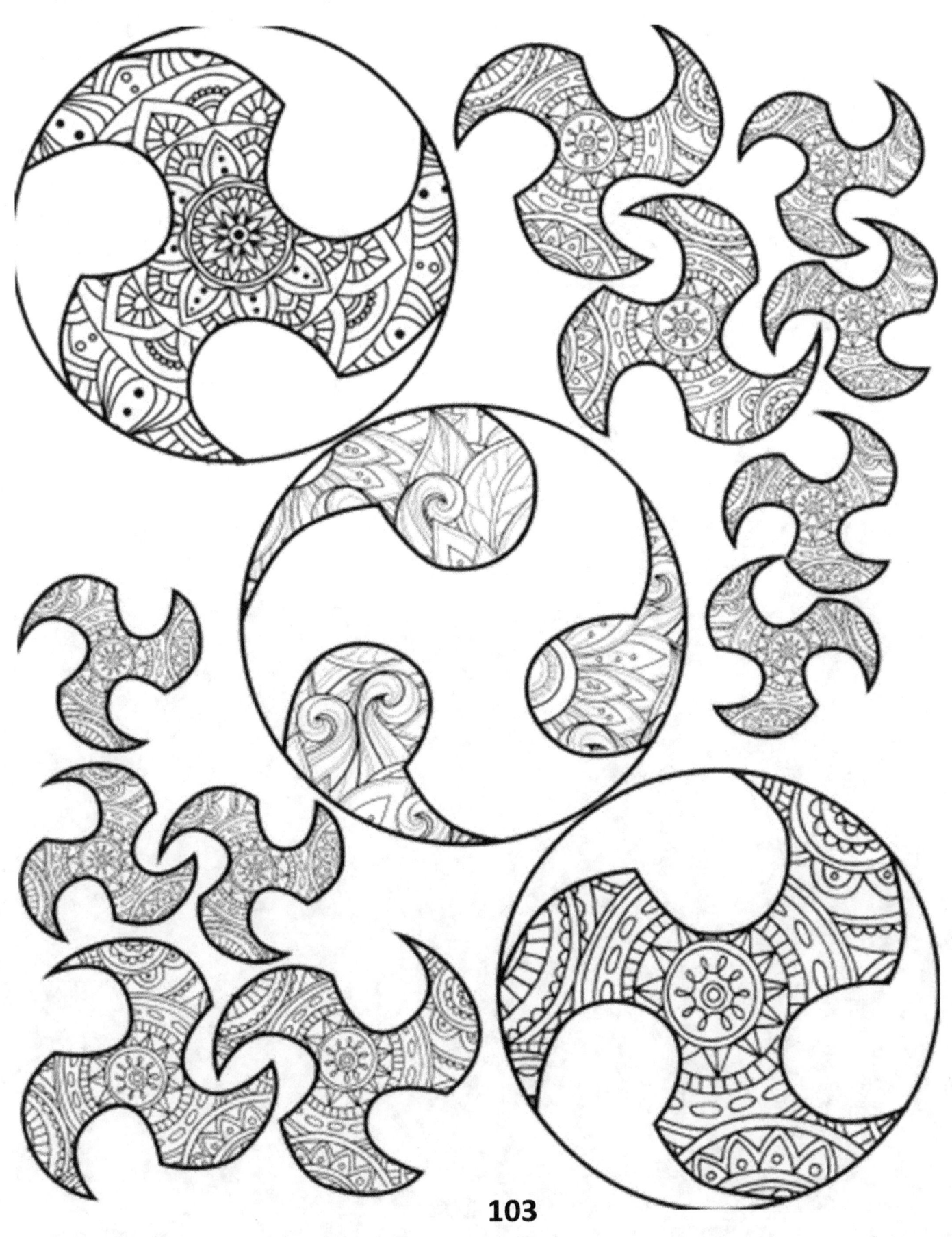